"Dr. Cline has an excellent biblical foundation with a great historical and inclusive perspective. This book helped me to understand the complex and challenging scriptures in the book of Revelation. I gained valuable insight and appreciate his diverse viewpoints on commentary."

—Cris Wagner, Men's Bible Study Leader and Teacher

"In this important book, Dr. Cline does a nice job of blending History, Archeology, and the spiritual with the Scriptural text of the book of Revelation. He provides a unique approach to reading and understanding the book so many people find confusing and bewildering. Without radical ideas or dramatic concepts, his approach brings the scriptural text to a level of understanding for the average person to relate and comprehend. This book is well worth reading and provides a helpful way to understand what St. John wrote for the Christian community of His day and how well it relates it to our time."

—Marvin Metzinger, MSA, Bible Studies Teacher, Catholic Bible School Graduate, Certificates from Dallas Theological Seminary, Ascension Press, and Augustine Institute.

"Thank you, Dr. Cline, for your unique insight. The book of Revelation can be very controversial no matter your faith. It can cause fear or instill great hope. Understanding what is told in Revelation confirms for us all that Jesus Christ is in everything from the beginning to the end of life. Dr. Cline knows this and has taken us through this final book of the Bible using wisdom and knowledge of scripture in a way that no matter who you are, what stage in life you are in, or what faith you profess, the journey is real and is now. Using references from the Old Testament to confirm their fulfillment in Christ in the New showed me that the scriptures are as relevant today as they have ever been. Dr. Cline explains this in a way that is understandable and unbiased. I recommend this book for anyone remotely interested in reading Revelation. Use it as a companion commentary as you study scripture. The journey is well worth it."

—Pam Schoenecker, Graduate of Denver's St. John Vianney Theological Seminary Lay Division Catholic Biblical and Catechetical School.

# Revelation Realist

# Revelation Realist

## Revelation About Jesus Christ From Jesus Christ

ERIC V. CLINE

*Foreword By Mark Eby*

RESOURCE *Publications* · Eugene, Oregon

REVELATION REALIST
Revelation About Jesus Christ From Jesus Christ



Resource Publications
An Imprint of Wipf and Stock Publishers
199 W. 8th Ave., Suite 3
Eugene, OR 97401

www.wipfandstock.com

PAPERBACK ISBN: 978-1-6667-1054-0
HARDCOVER ISBN: 978-1-6667-1055-7
EBOOK ISBN: 978-1-6667-1056-4

VERSION NUMBER 011223

We, Eric and Tina, dedicate this book about Jesus, realistically revealed, to Jacob, Jack, Luke, Vincent, Danielle, Libby, Alexander, and Jena.

Behold, children *are* a heritage from the Lord, The fruit of the womb *is* a reward. Like arrows in the hand of a warrior, So *are* the children of one's youth.

—Ps 127:3–4

If we do not experience His second coming, our children or their children may. I remind them to live boldly—push the envelope but live to talk about it. They are the arrows; may they fly straight and true.

The researches of many learned commentators have thrown much darkness upon this subject, and if they continue, we may be certain that we will soon know nothing about it at all.

—MARK TWAIN

# Contents

# Foreword

IN THE SUMMER OF 1961, I spent a week at the Christian Service Brigade Camp in Allegan, Michigan. I was eight years old, and this was my first week away from home.

The days were full of activities, and every evening all the campers would head over to the Fire-bowl for a bonfire, singing camp songs and hearing a Christian message. The camp director, Cap'n Green, delivered the message one particular evening. He told us a story about little Bobby, who grew up in a lovely Christian home with his parents and a couple of older siblings. In this story, everything was typical for a Saturday evening dinner, followed by some outdoor play, a bath, teeth brushing, prayers, and finally, bed. Nothing out of the ordinary. However, the next morning things were very different. Mom didn't wake him to go to church, and when he did wake up late, the house was empty!

Did his dad, mom, and his brothers go to church without him? Not likely; the car was still in the driveway.

Bobby noticed that breakfast looked partially prepared. To Bobby's horror, during the early hours of the morning, Jesus had returned! Jesus raptured the rest of his family, and he was (cue spooky music) *Left Behind*. After the story ended and as the fire was burning low, Cap'n Green asked his young charges if any of them wanted to accept Jesus into their hearts and get saved so they were assured a place in Heaven and wouldn't be left behind when Jesus came again. Naturally, my hand went shooting up, and that night I became a believer.

Though an awkward, distorted introduction to Christianity and Eschatology, the decision was genuine, and I have been walking with the Lord for almost sixty years now.

Since that memorable night, I listened to Dr. Jack van Impe's *Coming War with Russia* (1969); read Hal Lindsey's *The Late, Great Planet Earth*

(1970); *Satan Is Alive and Well on Planet Earth* (1973); and *The 1980s: Countdown to Armageddon* (1980). I didn't read Tim LaHaye's *Left Behind Series; I* only argued about them with other Christians.

When Tim LaHaye's *Left Behind* books were starting to come out, I reached the point that I was finished with the Dispensationalist "Pre-Mil" "Pre-Trib" Eschatology completely. For me, that entire system was untenable. A new parallel commentary, *Revelation: Four Views*, edited by Steve Gregg (1997), came out, and I read that. It is a commentary that compares the Historicist, Preterist, Futurist, and Spiritual interpretations in side-by-side columns.

I thought that, of the four views presented, the Preterist interpretation made the most sense to me. I also decided that my days of puzzling over the Revelation were behind me. Except for R.C. Sproul's book *The Last Days According to Jesus* (1998; Dr. Sproul was a Partial Preterist), I have steered away from eschatology books for over twenty years—at least all those written from a Futurist perspective.

So, imagine my delight when Dr. Cline asked me to read his manuscript of *Revelation Realist*. I asked him if his writing was of a futurist perspective with a written late date for Revelation, and he said that it was, sort of. So I graciously told him no thanks, not interested. But he was persistent. "This isn't like any other book on Revelation," he said. "This one is subtitled *"Revelation About Jesus Christ from Jesus Christ."* Well, that piqued my interest.

Revelation chapter one begins "the Revelation of Jesus Christ. . .". The "of" in that sentence does double duty: meaning both "about" and "belonging to." Since I've read precious little commentary on how the book of Revelation reveals Jesus, I asked, "So, you're not predicting future dates or events even a little bit?" "Nope, not at all. It's about seeing Jesus in the entire book, from the opening statement to the final "Amen." "OK," I said, "shoot it over. I'm not guaranteeing I'll read the whole thing, but I will at least start it."

I not only finished the manuscript, but I also enjoyed it. Dr. Cline had done prodigious amounts of study searching the Old Testament for examples of the symbols John used in describing his vision. It's easy to think that we have the liberty to interpret John's symbols however we want. That's how we get Russian Mi-24 Hind Helicopters out of scorpions (Rev 9).

In truth, Scripture does interpret Scripture, and by following this simple rule of hermeneutics, we begin to see what this vision meant and means to the churches. We see the parallels to the plagues of Egypt and the deliverance of Christ's people. We become familiar with the significance of numbers used in the Scriptures and what 200,000,000 might mean (not the Red Chinese Army).

We see the significance of the number "seven" and its repeated use. We read that John told to "eat the book" parallels both Jeremiah and Ezekiel, who "ate the Words of God." These are among the many other examples in Dr. Cline's book.

The Reformers developed a concept called the Sensus Literalis. Translated as "literal sense," we have to understand that the early Christians did not use "literal" the way we do today. They meant what we would probably call "literary." They believed that parables must be interpreted as parables, symbols as symbols, poetry as poetry, didactic literature as didactic literature, historical narrative as historical narrative. If one gets the genre of Scripture wrong, one will most likely get the interpretation wrong.

Martin Luther believed Christ is the Sensus Literalis of Scripture. He saw the whole of Scripture as revealing the messianic promise. Dr. Cline has taken a good step towards helping us understand this.

If you read this book and see the continuity of the Old Testament in the Revelation of Jesus to John, you will start to see both the Old and the New Testaments in the light of revealing Jesus. Revelation isn't about predicting the future—it's about revealing Jesus.

—Mark Eby

# Preface

I DO NOT CLAIM to reveal the "secrets" of Revelation or try and excite the reader with whimsical end-of-the-world proclamations. Revelation is one of the most influential books in Christian history. There are no secrets that reveal God's mysteries in Revelation, and I am not interested in spinning fanciful interpretations. While there is much to glean from extra-biblical literature, such as the Testaments of the Twelve Patriarchs and 4 Ezra, my focus is from *sola scriptura*, the Bible as the sole infallible source of authority for Christian faith and practice. It is the book of Revelation, not the book of Revelations. I try to steer clear of extrapolating the symbology beyond the limits of Scripture. The careful and courteous path for the devout Christian is to refrain from dogmatism when there is room for reasonable dissent. Scripture, especially in Revelation, is a foreign land, and reading the Bible is a cross-cultural experience, necessarily contextual. Our presuppositions that we bring the Bible influence our interpretation. Revelation was written to be read and understood, but to understand it within the first-century context, we must refrain from reshaping the context. Reading Revelation is neither simple nor easy but realizing Jesus is coming back is simply easy.

A symbolic world is created in Revelation to ensure that in good times and bad, Jesus is Lord. Jesus wins! Always. From the Greek word "*apokalupsis*", Revelation is a type of Jewish literature familiar to John's readers from the Hebrew scriptures. Revelation is prophesy, spoken to God's people, usually to warn or comfort them in a time of crisis. John did not stumble into a revelatory experience or hear God's voice by accident. We must believe that John readied himself to receive. It reminds me of the cliché, "When the student is ready, the teacher will be there." Revelation is a heavenly perspective on history considering its outcome, and it brings Old Testament prophesy to its climax. That is why in Revelation we will read parallel verses from the prophets, Ezekiel, and Daniel. John sent his apocalyptic prophesies to real people that John knew as he was known to the seven churches being addressed.[1] John does not actually learn anything new in his visions (no extra truths outside Scripture) and there are no gaps needing filled between the Old Testament and the New Testament. John was well versed in the Old Testament. There are many Old Testament quotations and references in Revelation. Jewish apocalyptic literature is communicated through symbolic imagery and numbers.

Ours is a material world. Our senses of the physical matter are seen, smelled, tasted, heard, and felt. Yet, there remains from day one, a spiritual realm, an aspect of reality that is nonphysical. There are immaterial spirits, including such things as deities, ghosts, angels, and demons. The human soul is among the immaterial spirits. The last book of the Bible is not a secret predictive code about the end of the world's timing. Events in Revelation, just as in Ezekiel and Daniel, apply to the first-century churches and throughout world history if the book's meaning is first anchored in the historical context of these first-century churches. They form a pattern of promise to all generations. In addition to being apocalyptic, Revelation is historical.

Jesus told the "end-times" story from atop Mount of Olives, a southern summit peak of 2,652 feet (808 meters) above sea level. Mount of Olives is east of Old City Jerusalem and is separated from it by the Kidron Valley. The end-times message, referred to as the Olivet Discourse, is recorded in Matt 24:1—25:46. Parallel passages are found in Mark 13:1–37 and Luke 21:5–36.

The biblical and external historical evidence is compelling, but the grand images will repeatedly "cock the eyebrow" of the modern Christian. John sees and hears things never experienced before, and he tries to explain and describe it the best he can using the language understood by his audience, and references what he does not know with "like what he does know or can imagine" and as God led his writing. Let's face it, John witnesses some really bizarre things! If you see something you have never seen before, the best you can do is say, "Well, it is like. . . " The words "as" or "like" occur more in Rev 9 regarding the fifth and sixth trumpet, than in any other chapter in the Bible. When John writes "like a leopard with feet of a bear and the mouth of a lion" we comprehend it was not an actual leopard, but John is describing a beast, unlike anything he has ever seen. John will compare visions with "like the Son of Man", "pure wool", "flame of fire,"

---

1. Dunn and Rogerson, *Eerdmans Commentary on the Bible,* 1539.

"fine brass," "a potter's vessel," "the sun," "chaff on a threshing floor," "the noise of many waters," "voice of the Almighty," "the noise of an army," "crystal," "blood," "an emerald," "frogs," and "grapes." Paul Decock writes "The symbol of blood is used in three different contexts: the blood of Christ (as saving power), the blood of the martyrs (as a cry for justice), and the blood of divine justice."[2] Once we disabuse ourselves of a supposed literalistic approach to Revelation, when we "let go" of how we think it should have been or should have occurred, we are in a better position to understand the book as John intended it, and of course, as inspired by the Holy Spirit.[3] Jesus painted pictures using parables and used metaphorical language. Aristotle said the mind thinks in pictures, and Pastor Warren Wiersbe commented that "It's by using metaphorical language that you turn people's ears into eyes and help them to see the truth."[4] Thus, the literature in Revelation is apocalyptic, historical, symbolic, and metaphorical.

Revelation has much to reveal to Christians of all generations but only in the context of John's time, place, and audience. We must discover the message of Revelation as it relates to the original readers who were in their last days just as we are now in our last days. But is that last day tomorrow, next week, or thousands of years from now?

Language is more than just words. The languages in one part of the world are very different from the languages in other parts of the world. Even within the United States the words forming sentences and the way the sentences are used vary significantly. For example, if I am fixin' dinner in Texas, a New Yorker may wonder if dinner is broken or they may also be fixing dinner with a "g." If I am surfing in Hawaii, someone else may be surfing on their computer in the office within the same state but not on the water as likely presupposed. "I'm all ears" is not taken literally. In some parts of the country, a pop is different than a soda. A person with a Texan drawl is clearly distinguished from a person with a New York accent. Figures of speech may exist universally but are universally different. A person may be busier than a one-armed paperhanger; another is working at Mach 3 with their hair on fire. "Walking like a new-born calf" might not be as relevant in New York as in Texas. "Nervous as a cat in a room full of rockers" is also descriptive and metaphorical. Prepositional language works well

2. Decock, "Symbol of Blood," 157.
3. Gentry, *Revelation Made Easy*, 98.
4. Wiersbe, *Developing a Christian Imagination*, 21.

in casual climates. We typically desire concrete absolutes in formal dialog. The reader of Revelation must be mindful of these presuppositions.

Genre influences how something is to be understood. We expect differences between the romance movie and the triller. Escape literature is different than the interpretive. We expect apocalyptic literature to have bizarre happenings with trumpets, plagues, stars, scrolls, and numbers. And we expect the animals to be strangely configured. God help us if we take all picture language literally. The metaphoric language is not to be taken literally while at the same time we cannot literally disregard the mere metaphor. The Lord's follower is a warrior, but their helmet of salvation is not an actual helmet. Being *like* a lion is different than *being* a lion. Consuming the Word through the intellect is different than eating a scroll.

It can rain cats and dogs, figuratively. It can figuratively rain three cats and four dogs. Numbers are symbolic or figurative in the book of Revelation as well as literal. The number seven is symbolic of perfection. The 144,000 is figurative of the tribes or symbolic of humanity.[5] Jesus symbolically portrayed as a Lamb with the figurative seven horns and seven eyes creates a much different image of our risen Savior. Six is half of a dozen but is the fullness of creation in Gen 1:26–31. Half of seven is three-and-a-half, broken from the perfect number seven. Three-and-a-half years is 1260 days but 1260 divided by the perfect seven is 180. If you turn 180 degrees, you turn completely opposite as one does in repentance from sin.

The immensity of one thousand is seemingly dwarfed if ten horns or ten diadems signify unlimited authority. Some treat all the numbers used in Revelation literally and some treat all of them as symbolic or figuratively. I treat some literally, some symbolically or figuratively, and some as either. Throughout this book I refer to "the adversary" using the Hebrew noun "satan" as a proper name "Satan." The three woes of the angels can be a literal three woes, and for Satan to be bound for one thousand years can mean being bound for a long time. Four horsemen and seven plagues are easier to conceptualize than the New Jerusalem at a height of 12,000 stadia, rising 1400 miles. What would that do to earth's orbit? Perhaps the New Earth could handle the New Jerusalem rising miles above in the absence of oxygen. Why not take the 1400-mile length by the 1400-mile width by the 1400-mile height literally? But then why would the New Jerusalem need a wall 216 foot thick or high? Robert Alcorn writes, "Mass and gravity are

5. For an intriguing perspective on the 144,000, see Huber, "Sexually Explicit?"

child's play to the Creator."[6] The throne of God is symbolic of power and authority, but a throne can also be an actual physical object. There are over 160 references to a throne in the Bible.

The book of Revelation, indeed the Bible, challenges us to look beyond the curtain through lenses borrowed from the world-wide, lost-and-found bin. We are to perform analysis of the biblical text in the language of its original author, and the grammar and lexicon of the day. If we interpret everything in Revelation as only symbolic, then nothing is real, and everything is "up for grabs" in terms of interpretation. One can spin the tail of fanciful interpretation around and sling heresy between book covers to intimidate some people into believing they are not smart enough to understand the Word of God. Yet God provides the sovereign gift of insight, "And He said to them, 'To you it has been given to know the mystery of the kingdom of God; but to those who are outside, all things come in parables, so that seeing they may see and not perceive, and hearing they may hear and not understand; lest they should turn, and their sins be forgiven them'" (Mark 4:11–12).

The preceding paragraphs are purposefully non-sequential; a random spilling of information about figures of speech and prepositional language to help us understand that much of the use of time in Revelation must be understood as non-sequential and non-linear. The Greek word *Chronos* is used to describe the more quantitative aspect of time, something of which us westerners are more accustomed to than of *Kairos*, the Greek word for a more qualitative aspect of an appropriate opportunity. This is especially important for western readers since *Kairos* is used almost twice as much in Revelation than is *Chronos*. Therefore, when we read, "there was silence in Heaven for about half an hour" (Rev 8:1), let us not set our chronometers for thirty minutes.

End-of-times alarmists might claim tomorrow or a particular date for Christ's return after reading, "Thrust in Your sickle and reap, for the time has come for You to reap, for the harvest of the earth is ripe" (Rev 14:15b). However, a good *Chronos*, here-and-now, example would be, "Today, if you will hear His voice, Do not harden your hearts" (Heb 4:7). Notice the difference between that and *Kairos* in the following question: At what time did the promise draw near to which God had sworn to Abraham, the people would grow and multiply in Egypt?" (Acts 7:17). Failing to acknowledge symbology, ignoring the context, and viewing time through western

---

6. Alcorn, *Heaven,* 491.

lenses will cause misinterpretation of Scripture, especially that in Revelation. There are more examples. In Dan 12:4, "seal the book until the time of the end. . ."; "Do not seal the words of the prophecy of this book, for the time is at hand" (Rev 22:10); "I watched till the beast was slain, and its body destroyed and given to the burning flame. As for the rest of the beasts, they had their dominion taken away, yet their lives were prolonged for a season and a time" (Dan 7:11–12). "For a season and a time" is a *prolonging of life granted to them,* a gloss that approximates the Aramaic. We must keep in mind that the Bible was translated from the original languages and even the best English translations do not always communicate the richness of the message. Dispensing expectation for perpetual chronological sequence is one of the first steps towards good hermeneutical exegesis. Here is an informative countdown sequence: Ten horns (Rev 12:3); nine beatitudes in Matthew (Matt 5:3–10); eight verses into the beginning and ending (Rev 1:8, 21:6); seven letters to seven churches (Rev 2–3); six plagues upon the earth (Rev 8–11); five months of continuous torture (Rev 9); four horsemen of the apocalypse (Rev 6); three unclean frog-like spirits (Rev 16); two witnesses (Rev 11); one worthy to open the scroll (Rev 5).

Some of the common numbers used in Revelation are mistakenly taken literally rather than symbolically as intended by John. Three is a number suggesting a few things or a limited time. Four suggests fullness. Seven represents perfection or perfect order. Ten typically indicates completeness or limit. Twelve is fullness or completeness, and thousand symbolizes a number too large to count. The symbolic colors are best explained in the text.

Millenarianism is the belief in a literal one-thousand-year reign of Christ.[7] "And I saw thrones, and they sat on them, and judgment was committed to them. Then I saw the souls of those who had been beheaded for their witness to Jesus and for the word of God, who had not worshiped the beast or his image, and had not received his mark on their foreheads or on their hands. And they lived and reigned with Christ for a thousand years" (Rev. 20:4). The thousand years, the millennia, can take on the three forms of interpretation held within the church today: premillennialism, amillennialism, and postmillennialism.[8] Each of them is significant but after the millennium is divided, dissected, and disputed, the three-way diversion

---

7. Horton, *Systematic Theology,* 920.

8. Millennium, Latin for "a thousand years" is also referred to as chiliasm from the Greek equivalent.

must be braided together to form the one consensus that Jesus is risen, and He has been given all authority in heaven and earth.

> Premillennialism: the belief that the second coming will occur before the literal one thousand years.

> Postmillennialism: the belief that the second coming/Christianization will occur after the nonliteral one thousand years.

> Amillennialism: not "no millennium" but the belief in the reign of Christ with the saints throughout the present long-period-of-time age from resurrection to return.

It is possible to interweave the three millennialism's with one or all five of the hermeneutical approaches, but the overlapping results are convoluted, insignificant, and rob a reader/learner of understanding, and serve only the writer's scholastic/academic preferences. That is why I offer only one-sentence definitions of each and join you, the reader, for the opportunity for continuous research and illumination.

The basic hermeneutical approaches to Revelation are futurist (most popular), historicist, preterist, idealist, and eclectic. I would like to suggest a sixth approach, "Realist". The serious reader of Revelation is a realist, a Revelation Realist. While these approaches are not necessarily incompatible at every point, they represent distinct views of the message and themes of Revelation.

> Futurist approach: The events of Revelation have not yet happened.

> Historicist approach: Some of the events of Revelation happened then, some are happening now, and some will happen in the future; a continuous history.

> Preterist approach: Most all the events in Revelation happened in the first century.

> Idealist approach: Timeless application of symbology to demonstrate the conflict between good and evil that recur throughout history.

> Eclectic: Apply the primary emphasis from each of the previous approaches.

> Realist: The events of Revelation are as real as is the call for us to repent and follow Jesus, trusting God in all things visible and invisible and to life in the world to come; God wins always and in all ways.

These approaches offer some interesting perspective on Revelation and force us to realize there are more than two sides of a coin (outside, inside, obverse or head, reverse or tail, smooth, patterned, mathematically infinite). We must interpret Revelation in an exegetically responsible manner, possible only after a seriously exhaustive study. Borrowing from Dr. Gorman, "How one reads, teaches, and preaches Revelation can have a powerful impact on one's own—and other people's—emotions, spiritual, and even physical and economic well-being."[9]

As we shall see in the different sections of Revelation, we must not miss the main points. Regardless of our millennial position, we can take comfort in the common thread through these approaches that Satan will finally be defeated, God takes care of His saints, and nothing more will be added to or subtracted from Revelation.

Second-century fathers Papias, Justin Martyr, and Irenaeus interpreted Revelation literally as if the events would take place in the future. This premillennial and futurist approach claims the events in Rev 1–19 would occur before the millennium, the thousand-year reign of Christ in Rev 20:1–8.[10] The earliest church overwhelmingly maintained a premillennial viewpoint. Millennialism, the belief in a thousand-year golden age paradise for saints on earth before judgment, eventually became controversial, and some understand it condemned by the Council of Ephesus (431) as a superstitious aberration.[11]

Origen, a third-century theologian in the Alexandrian church, rejected the futurist approach. Along with Tyconius and Augustine, Origen favored a more spiritual, idealist approach. Augustine spearheaded a more amillennial, idealist approach in which the thousand years represents the last period of history where the believers in Christ constitute the kingdom.[12] The Council of Ephesus in 431 accepted amillennialism as orthodox eschatological teaching, and it was later accepted as orthodoxy in Catholic and Protestant churches. The idealist approach set aside chronological or predictive issues and became a predominant view until the historical method was developed nearly a thousand years later.

Joachim of Fiore (1135–1202 CE) predicted a mass conversion of Jews before the return of Christ and that the Jews would reestablish themselves

---

9. Gorman, *Reading Revelation Responsibly*, xiii.

10. Blomberg, *Case for Historic Premillennialism*, 97.

11. Svigel, "Phantom Heresy," 107.

12. Blomberg, *Case for Historic Premillennialism*, 103.

in the Holy Land with theological importance as a distinct people.[13] This historicist interpretation in the progressive and continuous fulfillment of prophecy from Daniel's day to the end of the age is represented through the Reformation up to the current church age. Martin Luther was an amillennial historicist.[14] The historicist view of prophetic timing fulfillment can accommodate the premillennial, postmillennial, and amillennial views.

The preterist will agree with historicists that Christ did bring judgment upon Israel in 70 CE but will differ in believing that the coming of Christ in the Olivet Discourse and following the tribulation is future. Preterists believe that major Bible prophecies were fulfilled before the temple's destruction in 70 CE. Preterists are either postmillennial or amillennial.

The date of when Revelation was written is disputed to be near the end of the reign of the Roman Emperor Nero (54–68 CE) or the reign of Domitian (81–96 CE). There are good arguments and evidence for either date, but I lean towards the later-date approach, siding with Irenaeus's claim that John's vision was seen near the end of Domitian's reign. "But if it had been necessary to announce his name plainly at the present time, it would have been spoken by him who saw the apocalypse. For it was not seen long ago, [the apocalypse] but almost in our time, at the end of the reign of Domitian."[15] There is strong evidence found in Irenaeus's statement and much of the historical content of which John wrote about did not exist until the later date. Irenaeus was the disciple of the bishop of Smyrna, Polycarp, who was a disciple of John.

An early date approach is essential for the preterist, but the futurist can accept either date. I do not claim to be a preterist or a futurist. God has more to reveal to us in Revelation than historical events surrounding the destruction of the temple in 70 CE or whether the emperors are numbered from Julius Caesar (Suetonius system) or Augustus (Tacitus system).[16] I am a Revelation Realist.

Revelation is full of symbology and aside from the primary points, a particular stance is discretionary. However, an early or late date stance is helpful for continuity and the understanding of events before and after the destruction of Jerusalem and the temple in 70 CE. It is quite possible

---

13. McDermott, *New Christian Zionism*, 56.

14. Bigalke, "Revival of Futurist Interpretation," 46.

15. Irenaeus, *Against Heresies* 5.30.3.

16. This is explained in chapter 14—Cycle Five: Judgment on Babylon and Vindication of the Church (Rev 17:1–19:10).

the events happened before or shortly after the destruction of the temple with some events yet to happen in the future but woe to any who claim to precisely know God's plan.

The common thread throughout Revelation is that God is in charge and Jesus will return for his church, the believers and doers of God's will. The body of Christ. I differentiate between the church as a structure and the church of believers within context without capitalizing church. God is not confined by time, space, or gender so I also try to avoid using gender-specific pronouns. Where they must be used, they should not be capitalized.

Capital letters and gender pale miserably in defining God. It has nothing to do with the catastrophic trans-gender debacle but everything to do with complete reverence to Almighty God. Mortal humans can refer to God as him in biblical context and as it is in the inspired Word of God. However, as you will notice throughout this book, after I have proposed the various possibilities for certain events, I acknowledge from my knees that God is in charge and we must remain humble in our exegesis. God indeed created us male and female, but he ultimately transcends our human concept of gender.

It is not clear how or why John was sent to Patmos.[17] John may have been in exile. The Romans had a penal settlement on the island of Patmos to send people considered dangerous to good order. In John's early days, Emperor Nero was feeding Christians to the lions, Peter and Paul were crucified, and tradition has it that as John aged to his mid-80s, Emperor Domitian (81–96 CE), a profoundly insecure man who lived in morbid horror of being overthrown, is thought to have banished John to Patmos.[18] Domitian demanded that he be worshiped as "Lord and God"[19] and John's refusal may have prompted the banishment. Tertullian, the father of Latin theology and early Christian apologist, wrote that Domitian was much like Nero but that he later restored the Christians whom he banished.[20] However, Domitian was assassinated Sept 18, 96 and John made it to Ephesus after imprisonment under the reign of Emperor Nerva.[21]

Also disputed is the identity of John. He claimed to be a servant and brother but never claimed to be a prophet. There is little doubt he was Jewish,

---

17. Rogerson, *Commentary,* 1539.

18. Beitzel, *Baker Encyclopedia of the Bible,* 639.

19. Johnson, *Discipleship,* 39.

20. Espinoza, *Bible Dictionary,* Domitian Emperor.

21. Wentz, *Lexham Bible Dictionary,* Patmos.

and most claim he was the son of Zebedee, one of the twelve apostles and a disciple of Jesus. In that case, he would also be the author of the fourth gospel, John, as well as the epistles of John. Others, siding with the tradition of Papias as cited by Eusebius, claim him as John the Elder of Ephesus. The traditional view is that John the apostle is the author of the book of Revelation. Referring to him as John of Patmos is always a safe option.

Unless otherwise noted, I use "second coming" without application of any particular millennial viewpoint. The implication is about the return of Jesus Christ, "when He delivers the kingdom to God the Father, when He puts an end to all rule and all authority and power" (1 Cor 15:23–24). It would be risky and presumptuous for anyone to claim with absolute certainty, outside of Scripture, knowing God's plan for future events or even the "why" of recent events. The prophets of old were in the presence of the Lord's council and spoke with divine authority.[22]

Let us now enter this apocalyptic world and be transported by all the visions of Revelation and perhaps be shocked from our spiritual slumber.

22. "For who has stood in the counsel of the LORD, And has perceived and heard His word? Who has marked His word and heard *it?*" (Jer 23:18; also see 22:23).

# Acknowledgements

NONE OF US ARE where we are in life independent of others' influences, and I am surrounded by friends and family from whom I draw encouragement. Thank you. I felt particularly led to writing about Revelation after hearing endorser Cris Wagner criticize this last book of the Bible as being too complex and others shun Revelation and writings about Revelation because to them, it seems a far-fetched, "end-of-the-world" crisis book. I am profoundly grateful for the influence of "Pastor Phil," one of my favorite pastors who authored the cover endorsement for my book. For over a quarter of-a-century, he has unpacked the biblical message with consistent competence and a solid theological foundation. I have never heard from him a weak sermon, and he influences me to grow in the Lord continually. Air Force brother and former F-4 pilot Marvin Metzinger meticulously combed through my writing with his "Catholic" eye and offered numerous suggestions. His questions influenced me to search for answers and directly helped in my schooling. More than forty years ago in Germany, I enjoyed a weekend retreat alongside Christian brothers and sisters and admired Mark Eby's intellect. Mark and his wife Cindy were members of the church I attended. To me, Mark seemed like a walking encyclopedia. He could discuss various topics in detail, and he inspired me to at least attempt to broaden my horizon. Mark authored the foreword to my book and increased my sense of the work's seriousness. Our children have come to know Pam Schoenecker and her husband George as aunt and uncle. Pam dissected my writing and constructively challenged many of my thoughts. I value her Catholic and former Protestant perceptions and learnings. She influenced me to pay more attention to the details. My wife Tina and our children are always there for me.

# Abbreviations

*Hebrew Bible/Old Testament:*

| | |
|---|---|
| Genesis | Gen |
| Exodus | Exod |
| Leviticus | Lev |
| Deuteronomy | Deut |
| Joshua | Josh |
| Judges | Judg |
| Ruth | Ruth |
| 1 Samuel | 1 Sam |
| 2 Samuel | 2 Sam |
| 1 Kings | 1 Kgs |
| 2 Kings | 2 Kgs |
| 1 Chronicles | 1 Chr |
| 2 Chronicles | 2 Chr |
| Ezra | Ezra |
| Nehemiah | Neh |
| Esther | Esth |
| Job | Job |
| Psalm | Ps |
| Psalms | Pss |
| Proverbs | Prov |
| Ecclesiastes | Eccl |
| Song of Solomon | Song |

| | |
|---|---|
| Isaiah | Is |
| Jeremiah | Jer |
| Lamentations | Lam |
| Ezekiel | Ezek |
| Daniel | Dan |
| Hosea | Hos |
| Joel | Joel |
| Amos | Amos |
| Obadiah | Obad |
| Jonah | Jonah |
| Micah | Mic |
| Nahum | Nah |
| Habakkuk | Hab |
| Zephaniah | Zeph |
| Haggai | Hag |
| Zechariah | Zech |
| Malachi | Mal |

*New Testament:*

| | |
|---|---|
| Matthew | Matt |
| Mark | Mark |
| Luke | Luke |
| John | John |
| Acts | Acts |
| Romans | Rom |
| 1 Corinthians | 1 Cor |
| 2 Corinthians | 2 Cor |
| Galatians | Gal |
| Ephesians | Eph |
| Philippians | Phil |
| Colossians | Col |
| 1 Thessalonians | 1 Thess |

| | |
|---|---|
| 2 Thessalonians | 2 Thess |
| 1 Timothy | 1 Tim |
| 2 Timothy | 2 Tim |
| Titus | Titus |
| Philemon | Phlm |
| Hebrews | Heb |
| James | Jas |
| 1 Peter | 1 Pet |
| 2 Peter | 2 Pet |
| 1 John | 1 John |
| 2 John | 2 John |
| 3 John | 3 John |
| Jude | Jude |
| Revelation | Rev |

# Introduction

FOR PREACHING ABOUT JESUS, Rome imprisoned the beloved disciple John on the island of Patmos, modern day Turkey. In his later stage of life, John, the sole surviving disciple, addressed seven churches in seven cities on issues of persecution, compromised faith, wrongful wealth and worship, lascivious behavior, mingling, violence, and oppressive powers. In Revelation, the last book of the New Testament, Jesus-through-John floods the imagination with apocalyptic literature employing esoteric language. The supernaturally inspired book of Revelation articulates a pessimistic view of the present and pronounces warnings for the looming end of days. "Revelation's influence is noteworthy given the text's overall reputation for obscuring more than it actually reveals."[1]

1. Eusebius, *Ecclesiastical History*, as quoted by Lynn R. Huber in "Sexually Explicit?," 3.

# Section I—PROLOGUE (Rev 1:1–1:3)

"THE REVELATION OF JESUS Christ, which God gave Him to show His servants—things which must shortly take place. And He sent and signified it by His Angel to His servant John, who bore witness to the word of God, into the testimony of Jesus Christ, to all things that he saw. Blessed is he who reads and those who hear the words of this prophecy and keep those things which are written in it; for the time is near" (Rev 1:1–3). It is important to remember while reading through Revelation that John understood the Hebrew of the Old Testament and the Greek of the New Testament.

What other book in the Bible tells us that we will be blessed if we read that book? And this blessing is not symbolic or a parable—it is a clear-cut and observable promise from God. There are seven such blessings in this book, Rev 1:3; 14:13; 16:15; 19:9; 20:6; 22:7; and 22:14.[1] The words of Revelation are passed within the Trinity to an unnamed angel and then to John. God could accomplish all of this without angels but as Creator, God created creatures in the heavenly world and gave them tasks. Revelation describes the unfolding of history and the end of the world *as we know it.* Apocalypse does not mean "end of or destruction of the world. God destroys the ruling

---

1. Rev 1:3, "Blessed is he who reads and those who hear the words of this prophecy and keep those things which are written in it; for the time is near." Rev 14:13, "Then I heard a voice from heaven saying to me, "Write: 'Blessed are the dead who die in the Lord from now on.' "Yes," says the Spirit "that they may rest from their labors, and their works follow them." Rev 16:15, "Behold, I am coming as a thief. Blessed is he who watches, and keeps his garments, lest he walk naked, and they see his shame." Rev 19:9, "Then he said to me, "Write, 'Blessed are those who are called to the marriage supper of the Lamb!'" And he said to me, "These are the true sayings of God." Rev 20:6, "Blessed and holy is he who has part in the first resurrection. Over such the second death has no power, but they shall be priests of God and of Christ and shall reign with him a thousand years." Rev 22:7, "Behold, I am coming quickly! Blessed is he who keeps the words of the prophecy of this book." Rev 22:14, "Blessed are those who do His commandments, that they may have the right to the tree of life and may enter through the gates into the city."

powers of evil, not the world. When John says in verse one, "things which must shortly take place," he does not mean it is going to take place today, or tomorrow or soon as we might perceive time. The Greek translation of "shortly" is εν τάχει (*en tachei*), which means "great rapidity" or "with speed." The word tachometer is derived from εν τάχει. Things that must shortly take place mean that when it does occur, it will occur very rapidly. The roots of verse 1 are in Dan 2:28–30, 45–47. Daniel is speaking of the Kingdom of God that will come to pass in the latter days. Just as Joseph did in Egypt (Gen 40:8, 41:16), Daniel attributes his knowledge of the dream to God. God revealed to Daniel what astrology, magic, and the occult could not discover. The Holy Spirit moved John to write the book of Revelation.

The word "revelation" at the beginning of verse 1 is the translation of the Greek word αποκάλυψις (*apokalypsis*), from which we get the English word apocalypse. Apocalypse is revelation of what to expect, not the oft misused interpretation as "the end of the world." At the end of verse 3, we read ". . .the time is near," and the Greek word for "time" here is καιρὸς (*Kairos*), which means a season of time or opportune time, which is different from hour or *chronos* concerning a sequential time on a calendar or clock as we understand it today. A season of time would include the imminent return of Jesus Christ which can occur at any moment! In John's mind, the apocalypse does not happen at a specific location but is instead an "end-times" call for all to repent. Many readers fear the apocalyptic fervor of Revelation but aside from its primary message of "God's coming back, be ready," it serves to give hope for the righteous and warning for the rebellious.

Chapter One

# Greeting and Praise (Rev 1:4–1:8)

JOHN BEGINS GREETING THE seven churches in Asia. There were likely more than seven churches in the area, but these are the seven to which John was directed. These represent the real, physical churches of John's day, a number symbolic of perfection, and continue to represent churches throughout history. John is the human author, and in 1:4, his name appears for the second of four times in this book. John gets his messages from angels who get them from Triune God. We will see John's name again in verse 9 and verse 22:8.

The seven churches in Asia were in the Roman province of Asia Minor, part of modern-day western Turkey. The seas surrounding Asia Minor are the Black Sea, the Aegean Sea, and the Mediterranean Sea. Land east of Asia Minor is simply Asia or Asia Major. John is writing from the island of Patmos, just 75 km (46 miles) west of Ephesus on the coast of Asia Minor. His greeting of "Grace to you. . ." originates from God and includes the seven Spirits, the sevenfold ministry of the Holy Spirit from Isa 11:2, and is less likely a reference to the seven angels before the altar. [1] However, an argument can be made for the seven spirits before the throne to indeed be angels because John refers to the seven angels who stand before God in Rev 8:20. Yet, the sevenfold ministry of the One Holy Spirit is further emphasized indirectly with, "in the midst of the elders, stood a lamb as though it had been slain, having seven horns and seven eyes, which are the

---

1. See Isa 11:2, "The Spirit of the Lord shall rest upon Him, The Spirit of wisdom and understanding, The Spirit of counsel and might, The Spirit of knowledge and of the fear of the Lord."

seven spirits of God sent out into all the earth" (Rev 5:6). We will read about angels in powerful positions later. John no doubt knew of more than seven churches in Asia Minor but the number of congregations, seven, fits well with John's preference for the number as a symbol of perfection.

Jesus Christ is the witness and the firstborn from the dead and is first in the resurrection. Jesus is also "the firstborn of all creation" (Col 1:15). Jesus Christ has made us "kings and priests," which means Jesus has appointed us as a kingdom. This is evident in 1 Pet 6:5, "you . . . are being built up a spiritual house, a holy priesthood," and in verse 9, "a royal priesthood, a holy nation." We are as a kingdom to God and Father and are under the sovereign rule of Christ. We can appeal to God through a priest and personally because we have direct access to God as a priesthood. As children of God, our Father is always there for us.

So, bearing witness to whatever Jesus sees and hears from the Father and rising first from the dead, Jesus is coming to pass. John's vision is, "Behold, He is coming with clouds, and every eye will see Him"(Rev 1:7).[2] According to Gerald B. Stanton, the Greek word παρουσια (*parousia*) refers to the time of arrival of the Messiah, being alongside or in the presence of the Messiah, and not exclusively, "the second coming."[3] *Parousia*, as apparent in Zech 12:10—13:6, it is not the simple matter of arriving but the significant changes of that arrival. God's gracious Spirit produces repentance and humility in God's people. Thankfully, then, and now, Jesus has already freed us from our sins by His death on the cross. We are under the sovereign rule of Christ.

2. Jesus is coming: "Behold, he is coming" (Rev 1:7); "I am coming quickly" (Rev 22:7); I am coming quickly" (Rev 22:12); and "I am coming quickly" (Rev 22:20).

3. Stanton, *Kept From the Hour*, 20.

# Chapter Two

# Vision of Christ the Judge (Rev 1:9–1:20)

JOHN WAS A FELLOW victim in the persecution, trials, and tribulation under
Domitian rule in Rome. (This holds even with a preterist or early-date approach to Revelation if John was under the reign of Nero, except that I
would swap "persecution" with massacre). John was not the only one to
suffer the trials of God's people. A few examples include Moses wander-
ing in the desert, David fleeing for his life, kings persecuting Isaiah, and
Paul, along with many others in the New Testament, always catching grief.
But John's exhortation to endure and remain faithful runs throughout the
book of Revelation. If John the Apostle wrote Revelation, he was likely the
disciple whom Jesus loved.[1] John shared with his audience the distress, the
kingdom, and the endurance of Jesus.

Compare John's use of the word tribulation to that of Paul and
Barnabas's exhortation in Acts 14:22: ". . .strengthening the souls of the
disciples, exhorting them to continue in the faith, and saying, 'We must
through many tribulations enter the kingdom of God.'" The three goals of
apocalyptic literature are to console the audience, underline that God's sovereignty will prevail, and call the lost to convert and follow Jesus.[2]

John was in the Spirit on the Lord's Day, the first day of the week,
Sunday. He was caught up by the Holy Spirit. He was not demented. He
faithfully recorded genuine visions and revelations revealed by the angels
without any fabrications. In this spirit realm, John could see things of the
past, present, and future. Like Moses or Elijah—brought to the 'presence of

1. See John 13:23; 19:26; 20:2; 21:7, 20.
2. Cory, *Book of Revelation,* 96.

God' on Mt. Sinai or crossing the Jordan—God's 'cloud' engulfs him and brings John to God's presence where he hears God's voice. The loud voice told him, "What you see, write in a book and send it to the seven churches which are in Asia. . ." (1:7–8) and the names of the seven churches follow.

What John experienced in that moment, the presence of "the Alpha and the Omega, the First and the Last"(1:11), can only be described in the words given of the vision in 1:12–16. John saw seven golden lampstands (the first of many symbols in Revelation), which represent the seven churches, "the seven lampstands which you saw are the seven churches"(1:20), and the One in the middle is Jesus, the Son of Man. Son of Man alludes to Rev 7:13, "I was watching in the night visions, And behold, One like the Son of Man, Coming with the clouds of Heaven!" Imagine the menorah, the candelabrum having seven branches, with a central socket and three on each side. For some of the Jews in antiquity it was understood that the branches represented the five visible planets along with the sun and the moon. The symbolism here includes the seven-fold ministry of the Holy Spirit and what we shall see in Rev 1:20. But in addition to the seven churches, the lampstands are significant symbols of the churches in their principal function of giving light, especially with the glory of Christ at the center. The church is the lampstand, not the lamp.

Jesus appears in overwhelming glory, clothed in a fashion symbolic of His character. His garment (or robe) down to His feet is symbolic of His greatness as in Isa 6:1, ". . .I saw the Lord sitting on a throne, high and lifted up, and the train of His robe filled the temple." The wide golden belt (or band) around his chest refers to, perhaps, a towel He used after washing His disciple's feet (John 13:4–5). Or to the angel in Dan 10:5, "I lifted my eyes and looked, and behold, a certain man clothed in linen, whose waist was girded with gold of Uphaz!"[3] His hair white as wool (or snow) symbolizes the purity of His righteousness in the vision of the Ancient of Days recorded in Dan 7:9, "And the hair of His head was like pure wool."

In the vision described in 1:12–16, the eyes of Jesus looked different than what John remembered of Jesus's eyes before The Lamb's resurrection. Christ's eyes as John sees them now, are like "a flame of fire" (or fiery flames, burning fire). I think many of us could recall seeing someone or even ourselves having that penetrating look that would seem to burn right through someone or something. Penetrating eyes search for righteousness among the impure. From penetrating eyes to bronze feet, the deity of Christ, who

---

3. A gold-bearing region, mentioned in Jer 10:9; Dan 10:5, otherwise unknown.

has the attributes of God and is God, is the image John is witnessing. "He has put all enemies under His feet. . .all things are put under Him" (1 Cor 15:25–27). "His feet were like fine brass, as if refined in a furnace. . ." (Rev 1:15). I wonder if John noticed anything about the feet of Jesus when Peter, James, and John witnessed the Transfiguration of Jesus on the mountain? After all, they "fell on their faces and were greatly afraid" (Matt 17:6) after seeing that "His face shone like the sun, and His clothes became as white as the light" (Matt 17:2).

The point about the feet of Jesus being bronze could be drawn from another vision given to Nebuchadnezzar, king of Babylon, in the book of Daniel. King Nebuchadnezzar had a dream about a statue of gold, silver, and bronze but since having feet of clay and iron, the statue came crashing down and the pieces were carried away "like chaff on a threshing floor" (Dan 2:35). Human kingdoms cannot bear the weight on feet of clay, but God's kingdom, having feet of burnished bronze, are robust, tested, and strengthened by the fire. God's kingdom endures forever.

As we get into the book of Revelation, we will read about the destruction and fall of Babylon. It is essential to understand the difference between literal and symbolic Babylon, primarily because of some lesser-known facts about the history of Babylon. Babylon appears prominently in the biblical books of Daniel, Jeremiah, Isaiah, and Revelation. Babylon is a literal location currently 55 miles south of Bagdad, modern-day Iraq, and the ruins were reopened for tourism in 2009.[4] Babylon was first founded in 2300 BCE. The First Babylonian Empire or Old Babylonian Empire is dated 1880–1595 BC. King Hammurabi succeeded his father, Sin-muballit, and ruled Babylon within that time frame from 1792 to 1750 BC. "Hammurabi was one of the most notable kings of the first Babylonian dynasty because of his success in gaining control over Southern Mesopotamia and establishing Babylon as the center of his Empire. Babylon would then come to dominate Mesopotamia for over a thousand years."[5] Babylon eventually fell to Nabopolassar in 626 BC, creating the Second Babylonian Empire or Neo-Babylonian Empire from 626–539 BC before falling to Cyrus the Great. Babylon, according to Phillip Campbell, "was once a very important city back in the days of Hammurabi and the Sumerians. When Nabopolassar

---

4. This is after the 2003 invasion of Iraq when U.S. Forces built a military base on the ruins of Babylon. The United Nations cultural heritage agency UNESCO reported the base caused "major damage" to the archaeological site.

5. Podany, *Brotherhood of Kings*, 65.

emerged as the leader of those opposed to the Assyrians, Babylon would once again become important."[6]

It is in the Second Babylonian Empire or Neo-Babylonian Empire that housed the captives from Judea. Nebuchadnezzar II, son of Nabopolassar, held thousands of Jews captive there until Babylon fell in 539 BCE to Persian King Cyrus, a pagan, also known as the king of Babylon among many other titles such as "King of the Four Corners of the World." Ezra 1:2–4, records the edict of Cyrus for the Jews to return to Jerusalem (which is in Judah) and build a temple. One might rightfully claim that Cyrus's purpose was to enlist the gods of these people, in this case, the God Almighty, for his purpose and by doing so, the Jews were still under Persian influence. However, in the words of Prov 21:1, the Lord directed Cyrus's spirit like the "rivers of water; He turns it wherever He wishes." Cyrus is the only gentile named "His anointed" in the Bible.[7]

With Cyrus in command, Babylon became part of the Persian Empire which fell to Alexander the Great in 331 BCE, the third fall of Babylon. Subsequently, Babylon became deserted and forgotten; thus, there was no township of Babylon. Markus Stock writes, "Babylon, Macedon, and Carthage, are part of God's plan for the world: they ended at their appointed times after they had played their historic roles; they were full of warfare and bloodshed and led up to the Roman Empire."[8]

Consequently, some references to Babylon in Revelation are symbolic. Symbolically, as we shall see later in Revelation, any society, city, or nation seducing people away from true worship with false religions and sexual exploitation are forms of "Babylon." Babylon can therefore be Rome, Jerusalem, Egypt, or any other assemblage as such. In his farewell, Simon Peter refers to "she who in Babylon" as probably a reference to the church in Rome (1 Pet 5:13). Tiwald and Zangenberg write, "While Revelation vilifies 'Babylon' (and with this, certainly Rome) as the 'great whore,' it is not *first and foremost* concerned with Rome (and other places) *as cities*, but with ideas of wrong forms of worship."[9] I would also include the movements of Socialism, Marxism, Communism, and any other "–ism" taking our eyes off the Cross as Babylonian. Derived from the word Babel from the tower

---

6. Campbell, *Story of Civilization*, 26.

7. Isa 45:1.

8. Stock, *Alexander the Great*, 34.

9. Tiwald and Zangenberg, *Early Christian Encounters*, 263.

story in 11, Babylon is also a code word for humanity seeking to build without God.[10] We will learn more about a literal Babylon in Rev 14, 17, and 18.

Following John's vision of His feet, we read, "His voice as the sound of many waters" (Rev1:15). The sound of Christ's voice is also from another vision, but this vision is from Ezekiel. Ezekiel has a vision of God through living creatures with wings. This vision is a theophany (a visible manifestation to humankind of God) and, "When they went, I heard the noise of their wings, like the noise of many waters, like the voice of the Almighty, a tumult like the noise of an army; and when they stood still, they let down their wings" (Ezek 1:24). Imagine the roar of Niagara Falls or recall the intense surround-sound, movie-theater experience, or being near the launch of an Apollo rocket! His voice as the sound of many waters yet out of "His mouth went a sharp two-edged sword" (Rev 1:16). He will use His Word, the Word of God, to judge all the nations from cover to cover of the Bible. "For the word of God is living and powerful, and sharper than any two-edged sword, piercing even to the division of soul and spirit, and of joints and marrow, and is a discerner of the thoughts and intents of the heart" (Heb 4:12). According to Roman historian Vegetius, the sword was the Romans principal weapon of offense to be used in a stabbing action; "the point of the sword was more effective than its edge."[11] The type of sword (Gr., *rhomphaia*) mentioned here is a long, heavy sword mentioned five other times in Revelation.[12] This sword is a weapon of devastating judgment. However, William Barclay rightly proclaims the sword is not the fencing type and claims it is not long but rather a "tongue-shaped sword used for close fighting."[13]

I do not think it necessary to consider anything aside from the message's intent of the message: God's words will cut through rebellion in The Almighty's divine judgment as proclaimed in Isa 11:4, "But with righteousness, He shall judge the poor, And decide with equity for the meek of the earth; He shall strike the earth with the rod of His mouth, And with the breath of His lips He shall slay the wicked." God spoke creation; He can certainly speak judgment. Isaiah 49 mentions this sword regarding The Servant, Light to the Gentiles. *Rhomphaia* is only used seven times in the New Testament and only once outside Revelation in Luke 2:35. Of the four

10. Johnson, *Discipleship*, 298.

11. Allmand, "Particular Uses," 95.

12. Rev 2:12, 16; 6:8; 19:15, 21.

13. Johnson, *Discipleship*, 46.

gospel writers, Luke is more evangelistic, [14] and this sword can also be thought of as symbolic of the warrior nature of evangelism. [15]

In my narrative, I jumped (figuratively, not literally) from God's voice to God's tongue, skipping over that "He had in His right hand seven stars" (1:16). Like the seven lampstands, the meaning of the seven stars is revealed in 1:20, "The seven stars are the angels (or messengers) of the seven churches. . ." Note that the revelation of Jesus was delivered from the Father to the Son, to the Angel, to John, and to the messengers (angels). Further exegesis (interpretation) using cultural evidence would suggest another related certainty of the first-century mind and practice. The seven stars are symbolic. At that time, there were seven known planets, and the Romans often consulted astrological tables, and the Greek gods and goddesses lived high up in the sky on Mount Olympus. These gods could be found amongst the stars and planets. Might Jesus be alluding to the planets as well as the stars? The gods are only amongst the stars; the Almighty God holds the stars and controls everything, including the planets. Jesus is Lord of the Cosmos. "I am He who lives, and was dead, and behold, I am alive forevermore. Amen. And I have the keys of Hades and of Death" (Rev 1:18). The resurrection of Jesus Christ is the cornerstone of the Christian faith. I would imagine no one would snatch the stars from the right hand of Jesus, especially from what He makes known in John 10:27–28: "My sheep hear My voice, and I know them, and they follow Me. And I give them eternal life, and they shall never perish; neither shall anyone snatch them out of My hand" (emphasis mine).

14. Matthew is apostolic, John is prophetic, and Mark is pastoral.
15. Leon, *Seven Spirits*, 84.

# Section II –EXHORTATIONS TO THE SEVEN CHURCHES (Rev 2–3)

THE SEVEN CHURCHES ARE not symbolic; they are real, authentic places. The letters to the seven churches were applicable then, now, and in the future. Today's churches (and "church" as an organism of believers composing the body of Christ) would be wise not to neglect Christ's instruction to these seven churches. The modern-day church could exhibit all or some of the characteristics of the seven churches. Not every church has the same problems. Almost every one of the seven letters contain seven elements, and each of the seven letters are given to each of the seven angels.[16] Author Darrell W. Johnson makes a good argument that Jesus is speaking to the guardian angels of the church. These angels delivering the messages are genuine, supernatural beings—not preachers or a corporate "angel-ness" of each congregation. He argues that in Revelation, every use of the word angel refers to supernatural beings, never to human beings.[17] Jesus has a genuine care for the churches in His address, "I know your works" to each of the seven churches. Christ evaluates, rebukes, and commends; makes an "I will" statement; makes promises to those who overcome; and counsels to listen. Listen, and pay attention when Jesus speaks. Seek forgiveness and repent, turn from sin. When God speaks, man must respond and change or accept the consequences. The sequence of churches is thought to follow

16. The seven elements of each letter: 1) Christ commands John to write; 2) Christ identifies himself; 3) He praises the good works of the church (except for Sardis and Laodicea); 4) He admonishes the sins of the church (except for Smyrna and Philadelphia); 5) Christ calls for repentance or encouragement; 6) He exhorts the churches; 7) He concludes with a promise.

17. Johnson, *Discipleship,* 51–52.

the main stops on a circular road used as a postal route, and the church at Ephesus is the first stop for the messenger.[18]

Christ evaluates the seven churches in Asia Minor. The problems these seven churches faced are the same kinds of difficulties churches face today. Christ sees the problems and sins of the church perfectly; we see only imperfectly. If we could look at our church the way Christ does and heed The Son of God's solutions to the problems of the churches, we would learn what qualities Christ praises in a local church. Too many churches get wrapped up in growth strategies and the latest trends (especially in the extravagant misapplication of praise and worship) rather than about what Jesus Christ teaches. Christ founded the church and is the head and judge, and what Jesus says matters for eternity. We, as believers, are organisms of the church body. Injury to our own body summons immediate attention, and when God speaks to us as a church body, we must immediately seek God's saving grace.

When God speaks, we must respond. Christ alone will judge the churches. If we can learn from the messages of God's counsel in those seven letters to the seven churches, we can learn much that will help steer our churches, and the church, from failure and false teaching.[19]

18. Rogerson, *Commentary*, 1539.
19. Strauch, *Love or Die*, 1.

# Chapter Three

# Ephesus THE LOVELESS CHURCH (Rev 2:1–2:7)

EPHESUS WAS FOUNDED AS an Attic-Ionian colony in the tenth century BCE. Paul Trebilco writes, "From around 1000 to 550 BCE the city of Ephesus was located at the northern base of Mt. Pion, near the place where the Cayster river met the Aegean Sea."[1] John founded the first Christian community in Ephesus, but the church of Ephesus was established by Paul. Paul baptized some of the disciples there and apparently used Ephesus as his base of operations during his missionary journeys (Acts 19:1–41). Ephesus was once a famous and flourishing Greek city, a metropolis. John was likely able to see the temples, the theaters, the monumental municipal buildings, and many statues of pagan gods. The Temple of Artemis was the main temple in Ephesus. It was a Greek temple dedicated to the goddess Artemis. It was known less precisely as the Temple of Diana. After 70 CE, John would have seen the colossal statue to Titus, commander of the Roman forces that had burned the Jerusalem Temple. The apostle Paul left Timothy there as pastor to ensure proper teaching of the Christian doctrine (1 Tim 1:3). The Bible does not tell us if Timothy was martyred but if he was in Ephesus, it may have been the location of Timothy's martyrdom under Emperor Domitian or Nerva. However, Christopher Hutson writes, "If Timothy is in Ephesus . . . it's odd for him to say, 'all who were in Asia turned away from me' . . . so we might imagine Timothy in Iconium."[2]

The loveless church of Ephesus, the first of the seven churches, was not a social club. The church was busy doing. The church of Ephesus had

1. Trebilco, *Early Christians in Ephesus*, 12.

2. Hutson, *First and Second Timothy*, 171.

all kinds of ministries and programs. Stott, author and rector, summarizes the condition of the church as, "energetic in their service, patient in their suffering, and orthodox in their faith."[3] John praises their patience and abhorrence of the evil deeds of the Nicolaitans, a heretical group, probably having views like the teaching of Balaam and Jezebel. He commends them for their endurance in the face of deception by false prophets.

But the church was labeled "loveless" because they lost their first love— they had fallen out of pure and simple devotion to God, out of affection, out of intimacy. The church did well at discerning false teaching but apparently at the expense of loving others. They abandoned the love for people to ad- here to a strict and critical-of-others doctrine. Obedience to doctrine does not mean one has a love for the Lord. First John 3:14 instructs us to love the brethren and the first indication that the Ephesians lost their first love was when they stopped loving others.

Ignatius of Antioch also wrote a letter to the church of Ephesus about fifteen years after John had been there.[4] Ignatius, a disciple of John, en- dorsed the view that John, whom the Lord loved, wrote both the book of Revelation and the Gospel of John.[5] Ignatius also identified himself with people who suffered persecution and after declaring himself Christian be- fore a Roman magistrate he was fed to wild beasts around the year 110 CE.[6] He was martyred in Rome by the Emperor Trajan. Ignatius overcame and to those who overcome, Jesus promises they will eat from the tree of life.

3. Johnson, *Discipleship,* 56. John R. W. Stott served as rector of All Souls Church in London and was honored by *Time* magazine in 2005 as one of the "100 Most Influential People in the World." His many books, including *Basic Christianity* and *The Cross of Christ,* have sold millions of copies around the world and in dozens of languages.

4. Pagels, *Revelations, Visions,* 65.

5. Pagels, *Revelations, Visions,* 112.

6. Pagels, *Revelations, Visions,* 66.

Chapter Four

# Smyrna THE PERSECUTED CHURCH
## (Rev 2:8–2:11)

SMYRNA, THE SECOND OF the seven churches is dubbed the loveliest because the disciples there were living out their faith. The church in Smyrna was not rebuked by Jesus. There was a large Jewish population. It was also the persecuted church for that same reason. The Jewish synagogue in Smyrna was full of Jews who did not recognize Jesus as the Messiah and persecuted anyone who did. Persecution involved being tortured, boiled in oil, or fed to wild beasts—all for the entertainment of the "true" citizens of Rome. Jesus knew the *thlipsis*, the crushing pressure, the disciples were under in Smyrna.

Smyrna was a major seaport about 40 miles north-northwest of Ephesus and was an industrial center known for making wine. Whereas Ephesus had the temple of Diana, Smyrna had a temple dedicated to Emperor Tiberius, the second Roman emperor reigning from 14 to 37 CE. According to New Testament scholar Grant Osborne, Smyrna "beat out ten other cities for the privilege of building a temple to the emperor Tiberius."[1]

The initial settlement of Old Smyrna was founded around the eleventh century BCE. The birthplace of great writers such as Homer and Bishop Polycarp, Smyrna is present day Izmir, the third largest city in Turkey. "I know your works, tribulation, and poverty (but you are rich); and I know the blasphemy of those who say they are Jews and are not but are a synagogue of Satan" (Rev 2:9). What does Jesus mean by the last part of this verse?

1. Osbournen, *Hermeneutical Spiral*, 127.

Remember that in Smyrna there was a large population of Jews. There were Jews who had rejected the message concerning the coming of the Messiah. They created a cult of sorts where they mixed their Jewish faith along with other religious practices which was fine in the Roman Empire if the priority of worship was given the emperor. Though these Jews professed to worship God, their opposition to Christians showed that they were in fact under the power of satanic darkness.[2] Their synagogue was a synagogue of Satan.

The Romans once considered Christianity a part of Judaism and permitted the Jews to worship whomever if they also worshiped the emperor. When some of the Jews converted to Christianity and the Christians refused to worship the emperor, Christianity was no longer a religion under the shelter of Judaism. Christianity became a crime and Christians were punished by the non-converted Jews and the Romans.

The church in Smyrna is "rich" in God's glory with God's mercy, love, peace, joy, salvation, forgiveness, fellowship, provision, and God's comfort. Otherwise, the Christians of Smyrna were impoverished because they would dare not employ themselves in the trades, the main source of income. Membership in the trade working environment often involved gatherings having food which was sacrificed to idols and rituals of worship to the Roman emperor. In the letter to the church of Smyrna, John tells them to not fear, and to endure the testing and probable imprisonment to the point of death. Their tribulation for ten days in Rev 2:10 may be an allusion to the story of Daniel and his friends, who were tested for ten days when they refused to eat food dedicated to idols (Dan 1:12–15; 5:3–4).

In the years after John's death, people were continuing to witness the end times of which John wrote. Gentile-to-Christian-convert Justin was arrested in 165 CE, charged with being a Christian and, refusing to make sacrifice to the gods, was whipped and beheaded along with six of his students.[3] Shortly before that in 155 CE, Irenaeus's eighty-six-year-old-mentor, Bishop Polycarp, was "arrested by the authorities and brought before the proconsul in the arena during a festival. When ordered to deny his faith, Polycarp responded, 'For eighty and six years have I been his servant, and he has done me no wrong, and how can I blaspheme my King who

---

2. 2 Cor 4:3, 4: "But even if our gospel is veiled, it is veiled to those who are perishing, whose minds the god of this age has blinded, who do not believe, lest the light of the gospel of the glory of Christ, who is the image of God, should shine on them."

3. Pagles, *Revelations, Visions*, 110.

has saved me.'"[4] Many other "confessors of Christ" were killed by various "entertainment" methods and in compliance with Roman law. Witnesses were becoming more aware of what John predicted in his writings commissioned by Jesus. "Be faithful until death, and I will give you the crown of life" (Rev 2:11). Those who overcome will not be hurt by the second death.

4. Ascough, *Religious Rivalries*, 9.

Chapter Five

# Pergamum THE COMPROMISING CHURCH
## (Rev 2:12–2:17)

THIRD OF THE SEVEN churches is the compromising church, the church in Pergamos or Pergamum, the city of the sword—one of the few cities to which Rome had given the power to inflict capital punishment. It is home to one of the oldest temples in Asia Minor devoted to emperor worship, the temple of Trajan.

Founded in the Hellenistic period, around 280 BCE, the main sites of ancient Pergamum today are to the north and west of the modern city of Bergama, an Izmir Province in western Turkey. In 123 CE, Emperor Hadrian built upon the efforts of Emperor Trajan to develop the city into a metropolis which elevated it above its rivals, Ephesus, and Smyrna.

Pergamum was a prominent city and pagan religious center.[1] People could seek medical care from Asclepius, a Greek god of healing. The famous medical doctor, Galen, who we will read about in the church of Laodicea, was from Pergamum.

Pergamum was about thirty-five miles north of Smyrna and about twenty miles north of the Mediterranean Sea. The city had one of the largest libraries in the world and a famous school of sculpture. This important learning center was famous for parchment called *pergamena*. Parchment is durable writing material made from the skins of sheep, goats, or calves

---

1. Pergamum was an important religious center where pagan cults of Athena, Asklepios, Dionysus, and Zeus were prominent.

unlike less durable papyrus which was made from the papyrus plant.[2] The city was also known for its silver mines, textiles, and agricultural work.

Like Ephesus and Smyrna, Jesus was manifest before the Pergamum church and had a few things against them for false worship. They were at the center of Caesar worship, being the first to build a temple to Augustus. The entire area was Satan's throne, probably a reference to the monumental altar to Zeus or to emperor worship. "These things says He who has the sharp two-edged sword: 'I know your works, and where you dwell, where Satan's throne is. And you hold fast to My name and did not deny My faith even in the days in which Antipas was My faithful martyr, who was killed among you, where Satan dwells. But I have a few things against you because you have there those who hold the doctrine of Balaam, who taught Balak to put a stumbling block before the children of Israel, to eat things sacrificed to idols, and to commit sexual immorality. Thus you also have those who hold the doctrine of the Nicolaitans, which thing I hate'" (Rev 2:12–15).

Jesus warned the Christians in Pergamum of judgment unless they repent (Rev 2:16). However, those who conquer by exercising repentant faith will receive "hidden manna" (Rev 2:17), probably an unfailing supply of heavenly, spiritual food. Christ promised to sustain His people just as He sustained Israel with manna in the wilderness (Exod 16). The Pergamon Christians are also promised a white stone with a name engraved on it (Rev 2:17). In those days, if you were tried for a crime, a white stone placed into a jar signified acquittal. The color white is symbolic of victory and purity. Jesus is likely promising something of great value to faithful Christians. On this stone is a "new name," perhaps a reference to a new status conferred by Jesus just as a new status went with a new name for people such as Abraham (Gen 17:1–8). Those who persevere are forever acknowledged as children of God.

I agree with author D. W. Johnson that Jesus would not be welcomed there by the chamber of commerce, city council, or the welcome wagon.[3] The atmosphere was completely averse to Christian testimony. But what Jesus was telling them by way of the letter delivered by the messenger was that the Son of God hated the doctrines of Balaam and the Nicolaitans and rebuked the church for compromising their stand for the truth. This is the origin of "the compromising church." The Christians accommodated their faith to the demands of the wider culture. Balaam, the false prophet, was

2. McDowell, *Evidence*, 22.

3. Johnson, *Discipleship*, 77.

hired by the kings of the Midianites and the Moabites to curse the children of Israel (Num 22–25). Those who followed Balaam as recorded in Numbers used Midianite women to seduce the men of Israel and lead them to worship other gods. Balaam failed to curse the children but in chapter 31 of Numbers we learn that he influenced the Israelites to intermarry with the heathen and participate in idolatrous worship which is exactly what was happening in Pergamum.

Civic and religious life were so entwined that the Christians were caught up in the pagan feasts, immorality, and idolatrous worship. Christ commended the Christian Ephesians for hating the Nicolaitans but the church at Pergamum embraced the sect. The Nicolaitans conformed to the Roman culture of making sacrifices to their gods and persuaded the Christians to comply or suffer persecution. This is unrighteous compromise. Today, it is sometimes difficult to distinguish between the church and the world. James Davison Hunter writes, "the actual vitality of American Christianity's cultural capital today rides almost exclusively among average people in the pew rather than those in leadership, on the periphery not the center of cultural production, in taste that run to the popular rather than the exceptional . . . and almost always toward the practical as opposed to the theoretical or the imaginative."[4] In other words, like the church of Pergamum, many of today's churches are accommodating their purpose with the entertainment demands of the wider culture. God's people are supposed to be in the world, not of the world and yet set apart from the world (Matt 24:14; John 1:29; Ps 4:3).

The one bit of praise from Jesus to the church of Pergamos was that some held fast to their faith in Jesus amidst Satan's throne and the killing of Antipas. In addition to the promise of white stones and hidden manna, Jesus promised to come quickly and fight against those still holding to the doctrine of the Nicolaitans. It is worth repeating that messages to the seven churches in the first century are just as applicable for today's churches, but they are not a panorama of church history.

---

4. Hunter, "Cultural Economy of American Christianity," 79.

## Chapter Six

## Thyatira THE CORRUPT CHURCH
## (Rev 2:18–2:29)

THE FOURTH CHURCH IN the messenger's circuit, Thyatira, is the most difficult to interpret because there is not much archeological information. Thyatira became part of the Roman Republic in 133 BCE and was the center of worship of Apollo and apparently Caesar since both were believed to be the son of Zeus. In Rev 2:18, Jesus purposefully identifies as "Son of God," countering the action of Emperor Domitian naming his son, "son of god."

Thyatira was on the borders of Lydia and Mysia (location of Mt. Olympus), about 40 miles east-south-east of Pergamos and a similar distance north-east of Smyrna. Thyatira was a prosperous commercial center with many of its inhabitants involved in trade and manufacturing activities such as linen and leather workers, tanners, bakers, potters, bronze smiths, and shoemakers. If you were not part of those groups, it would be hard to make a living. The problem was that belonging to that industry also involved engaging in their social activities which included pagan worship. For example, tradesmen meetings would typically include pagan sacrificial meals and to not participate would endanger one's membership in that group. The tables will turn, however. Imagine the iron of the bronze smiths breaking the vessels of the potters. Jesus reminds us of Mic 4:1–5, that the people of God will rule over the nations and even judge them. We will receive the "morning star," Jesus Christ.

Christ directed the longest letter to this church. It is one of the most severe letters because of the severity of adultery, sexual immorality, and idolatry. They have been led into an unholy alliance with pagan doctrine and practice. They allowed Jezebel "who calls herself a prophetess, to teach and seduce My servants to commit sexual immorality and eat things sacrificed to idols" (Rev 2:20). Jezebel taught this as being justified while also worshiping Christ. She may have been one holding to "the doctrine of the Nicolaitans" (see Rev 2:15). This is where Thyatira gets named the "corrupt church" and why this letter is so severe. Jesus uses the name Jezebel perhaps because the woman justifying compromise in Thyatira had all the marks of the Jezebel in the Old Testament (1 and 2 Kings). No true Christian recognized her as a prophet and John mockingly associated her with the Canaanite queen who induced her husband Ahab, to worship idols and even try to kill the prophet, Elijah.

Jesus gave Jezebel time to repent but she did not. Jesus promises to kill her children, all those who follow her adulterous ways, with death. First and Second Kings records that she was eaten by dogs as told through Elijah's prophesy. The great tribulation in 2:22 refers to general suffering, and not the great tribulation Jesus mentioned in the Olivet Discourse. The penalties in 2:21–23 are immediate and not held for the end of times.

There are parts of a picture in this letter to the church in Thyatira to help answer the obvious question of why one should stay loyal to Jesus in this marketplace. I refer to author D.W. Johnson's story about the pastor who thwarted proposition from a temptress by showing her a picture of his wife and proudly proclaiming, "I belong to her." [1] In similar manner, a "picture" of Jesus is delivered to the church of Thyatira. In Rev 2:18, Jesus gives the title, "Son of God" followed by the One "who has eyes like a flame of fire" and "whose feet are like burnished bronze." Jesus gave her, Jezebel, time to repent but she was unwilling. Jesus tells the church "I will give to each one of you according to your works" (Rev 2:23b). The picture is completed with the theme of kingship from Ps 2, "And he who overcomes, and keeps My works until the end, to him I will give power over the nations—He shall rule them with a rod of iron" (Rev 2:26–27). Reference to a male child, not from Jezebel, who was to rule all nations with a rod of iron is made in Rev 12:5.

The message to the church at Thyatira tells us to persevere in the Lord's work whether anyone takes notice. The Christians of Thyatira were praised for their works of love, service, faith, and patience. Jesus always sees those who serve the Son of God, and Jesus will give to each of us according to our works. In the last part of this message in Rev 2:28, Jesus will also give the

---

1. Johnson, *Discipleship,* 92–94.

morning star, which I interpret messianically to mean the second coming of Christ, the "light that shines in a dark place" (2 Pet 1:19), "A star shall come out of Jacob" (Num 24:17), and "I am the Root and the Offspring of David, the Bright and Morning Star" (Rev 22:16b).

Chapter Seven

# Sardis THE DEAD CHURCH (Rev 3:1–3:6)

THE FIFTH CHURCH, SARDIS, was the largest and wealthiest of the seven and like the church at Ephesus, it too had lots of programs, and yet Jesus says, "you are dead" (Rev 3:1). Their behavior compared to the way many people celebrate Christmas and Easter today—lots of ritualistic shopping and procedure but they forgot what it is all about. The church of Sardis earned the name, "the dead church" because they were essentially going through all the motions without genuinely practicing faith. Like the church in Smyrna, there was a large Jewish population.

Sardis was about thirty miles southeast of Thyatira and fifty miles east of Smyrna. The city is located at the foot of the Tmolos mountain range, where the Pactolus River runs through the Hermus plain. Founded in the third century BCE, Sardis was once the capital of Lydia and the place where gold and silver coins were first struck.[1] Most of the city practiced pagan worship and it was known for its loose living. The church may have had a strong testimony for God in show, but God sees all and at Sardis there was little genuine spiritual life and power. The same can be said for any modern-day churches who love systems more than Jesus, form more than life, or material rather than spiritual.[2]

Unlike the growing metropolis of Pergamum, Sardis was in a period of decline because of the 549 BCE invasion by the Persians and the 214 BCE invasion of the armies of Antiochus the Great. Richard Ascough writes that it is unknown what the Jews of Sardis thought about "the three great

1. Mounce, *Book of Revelation*, 92.
2. Barclay, *Letters*, 87–88.

revolts of 66–70 and 132–35 in Judea and 115–17 in Egypt, Cyrenaica, and Cyprus."[3] The devastating earthquake of 17 CE was not any help. Sardis did not watch for the enemy and the messenger is warning that if Sardis does not heed Christ's warnings, "I will come upon you as a thief" (Rev 3:3b). Jesus will come unexpectedly with devastating judgment. There are some there who Jesus will confess before God because they remain true to Christ and their names can never be erased from the book of life (3:4–6). Our salvation does not depend upon works but by grace alone that produces a repentance in man that is expressed by works that follow. "Thus also faith by itself, if it does not have works, is dead" (Jas 2:17).

There are a few in Sardis who have not defiled their garments, a reference to the sixth plague (Rev 16:12–15) of those walking naked in shame. The worthy will walk with Jesus clothed in white garments.

The lessons for Sardis can certainly be applicable in today's church. There are many true Christians who will live forever, and their names will not be blotted from the Book of Life, an allusion to the heavenly roster of the holy ones in Rev 20:12. "He who overcomes shall be clothed in white garments, and I will not blot out his name from the book of life"(Rev 3:5). The mark of true Christians is revealed in the repentant lives they lead of loving God and fellow man. True Christianity is without denomination. True Christianity is not a walk in the park wearing a crown but a buckling of the knees before the cross. Conversely, the nominal Christian is in name only, perhaps religious without relationship, and worldly obedient yet wayward of The Way.

3. Ascough, *Religious Rivalries*, 19.

# Chapter Eight

# Philadelphia THE FAITHFUL CHURCH
# (Rev 3:7–3:13)

FOUNDED IN THE SECOND century BCE, the church in Philadelphia, present-day Alasehir, Turkey, was located about twenty-five miles southeast of Sardis, and its location was ripe for wine production, which was its chief industry. Along with Sardis, Philadelphia also experienced the devastating earthquake of 17 CE. Philadelphia experienced another setback in 92 CE when Domitian ordered the destruction of half of their vineyards. The vine edict of Domitian also prohibited the planting of new vineyards to allow the fields to be used for growing corn during the famine. This edict remained in effect for 188 years.[1]

Philadelphia was named after a king of Pergamum, Attalus Philadelphus, who was an accomplished military commander. Otherwise, Philadelphia is from the Greek φιλεω (*phileo)* meaning "to love" and αδελφος (*adelphos*) meaning "brother."[2] This church and the church in Smyrna are the only two of the seven that Jesus did not rebuke.

The message addressed to the sixth church, Philadelphia, has the unusual characteristic of being almost entirely one of praise. Let Scripture alone describe the joy Jesus must have felt dictating the message to faithful church with the open door:

1. Jones, *Empire Domitian*, 78.

2. Brotherly love is used in Rom 12:10; 1 Thess 4:9; Heb 13:1; 1 Pet 1:22; and 2 Pet 1:7.

> And to the angel of the church in Philadelphia write, 'These things says He who is holy, He who is true, "He who has the key of David, He who opens and no one shuts, and shuts and no one opens": "I know your works. See, I have set before you an open door, and no one can shut it; for you have a little strength, have kept My word, and have not denied My name. Indeed I will make those of the synagogue of Satan, who say they are Jews and are not, but lie—indeed I will make them come and worship before your feet, and to know that I have loved you. Because you have kept My command to persevere, I also will keep you from the hour of trial which shall come upon the whole world, to test those who dwell on the earth. Behold, I am coming quickly! Hold fast what you have, that no one may take your crown. He who overcomes, I will make him a pillar in the temple of My God, and he shall go out no more. I will write on him the name of My God and the name of the city of My God, the New Jerusalem, which comes down out of heaven from My God. And I will write on him My new name (Rev 3:7–12).

This passage is in stark contrast to the messages to Sardis and, as we shall see, Laodicea. The church in Philadelphia faced much opposition from the culture. Just as there were Jews in Smyrna "who were not," the same problem existed in the church of Philadelphia. These Jews by heritage only were not the people of God which distinguished them from the Jewish followers of Christ.

The non-Christian Jews formed the synagogue of Satan and were likely the ones who expelled the Jewish Christians from the synagogue, placing them without the religious protection Rome gave to the Caesar-worshiping-Jews. As we will see that the "mark of the beast" is not necessarily a literal mark. "I will write on him the name" can be symbolic, meant as belonging to God, and is more of a *seal* than a *mark*. Blackwell writes, "'Seal/sealed' (Gk. *sphragis/sphragizo*) is used exclusively as a positive term for the faithful (7:2, 3, 4, 5, 8; 9:4); and, 'mark' (Gk. *charagma*), is used exclusively as a negative term for those who resist God (13:16, 17; 14:11, 14; 16:2; 19:20; 20:4)."[3] The mark of a killer, pedophile, or thief is just as much embedded under the skin as is the seal of the saving grace of Jesus Christ and redemption for a disciple—it is the character of such. Jesus promises the Philadelphia Christians who endure will be made a pillar in God's temple. Twentieth-century missionary, Jim Elliot, famously said, "He is no

---

3. Blackwell et al., *Reading Revelation in Context*, 77.

fool who gives what he cannot keep to gain what he cannot lose." We come into this world with nothing but the inheritance we can have in Heaven can never be destroyed.

# Chapter Nine

# Laodicea THE LUKEWARM CHURCH
# (Rev 3:14–3:22)

Laodicea was founded by a Greek king of the Hellenistic Seleucid Empire, Antiochus II, and named after his wife Laodice. Laodicea is forty miles southeast of Philadelphia on the road to Colossae. Over that road to Colossae was carried Paul's epistle to the Colossians where they were told that Christ is "the image of the invisible God, the firstborn of all creation" (Col 1:15), and as "the beginning, the firstborn from the dead" (Col 1:18). My point is that Paul, a generation earlier, had concern for the spiritual state of the Laodicean church and the message to this church is the most scathing of the seven when Jesus essentially tells them "you make me sick" in Rev 3:16. The only place other than Rev 3:14, "These things says the Amen" where Amen is used as a name is Isa 65:16, where "God of Truth" can be more literally translated "God of Amen" since Amen is derived from the Hebrew āmēn, which means "certainty," "truth," and "verily."

Probably the best known of the seven messages comes to us with," Behold, I stand at the door and knock" (Rev 3:20a). You may recall seeing the artists' popular rendition of Christ standing outside the door and the door handle is only accessible from the inside. However, this comes to us sandwiched between Jesus saying, "I will vomit you out of My mouth" (Rev 3:16) and "I will come in to and dine with him, and he with Me" (Rev 3:20b). Clearly, Christ is not happy with lukewarm Christians: "you are neither cold nor hot. I could wish you were cold or hot. So then, because you are lukewarm, and neither cold nor hot, I will vomit you out of My mouth" (Rev 3:15–16). Consequently, the church of Laodicea earned the name, "the lukewarm church." Some commentaries attempt to explain the church being lukewarm by using local imagery of hot and cold-water merging. Laodicea received hot water from Hierapolis to the north, and from ten miles east the cold water came from Colossae. Merging the two would make for lukewarm water. Osborne writes, "The city had to pipe it in, and when it arrived it was lukewarm and so mineral-laden that drinking it could cause an upset stomach."[1]

However, the aqueduct supplying water to Laodicea came from the south. David Croteau writes, "Denizli had a hot spring and was located about six miles south of Laodicea. The Laodiceans constructed an aqueduct that ran from Denizli to Laodicea providing water for the citizens."[2] Laodicea had water access from two rivers and two springs, the main one located six miles south of the city. A sophisticated network of channels, pipes, reservoirs, and fountains supplied the city's needs.

It is always important to interpret Scripture using a handful of valid resources, first of which is other Scripture followed by context. Without other Scripture, we find various commentary about lukewarm water and to that I will add another. Perhaps Jesus is telling us to be one way or the other in our faith but not from an undeclared or compromised "middle" position, especially given the Jews "who are not Jews" and are in the "synagogues of Satan" as we read about earlier in the other churches. Jesus does not want half-hearted worship. Be one or the other, hot, or cold. Pick a lane!

The more important points in Rev 3:14–22 are the references to the naked, poor, and blind, and those references are supported by other scriptures as well as context. For example, the Laodiceans claim they are rich and have need of nothing. Historical evidence informs us that under Roman rule they indeed had become wealthy enough to rebuild their city without any outside help after it was destroyed by an earthquake in about 60 CE.[3] It is entirely possible for someone to be so secure in their wealth and or their self-sufficiency that they are convinced they do not even need God. In this regard, they are poor because they are without the riches of Christ. They are spiritually bankrupt, "the poor have the gospel preached to them" (Luke 7:22). The Laodicean believers lacked anything of spiritual advantage despite their possession of material benefits. Steve Gregg writes, "Wealth has a way of imparting a false sense of self-sufficiency—the very antithesis of

1. Osborne, *Revelation Verse by Verse*, 63.
2. Croteau, *Urban Legends*, 229.
3. Osborne, *Revelation Verse by Verse*, 64.

the beggarliness of spirit commended in the Sermon on the Mount" (Matt 5:3).[4] Yet to anyone hearing and overcoming mediocrity and independence from God, Jesus "will come in to him and dine with him, and he with me" (3:20).

As a reference to Adam and Eve in the Garden, they are also naked and should be covered with white garments (righteousness) so that "the shame of your nakedness may not be revealed" (Rev 3:18). They were spiritually blind like the man disciplined for disobedience, "you shall grope at noonday, as a blind man gropes in darkness" (Deut 28:29). What is interesting about the blindness is that Laodicea, as a wealthy city with its own textile industry (wool) and robust banking system, it also had its own medical school and either produced or distributed an eye ointment known as "Phrygian" powder. Laodicea was famous for this ointment, but it was powerless to cure spiritual blindness.[5] Galen, a physician, surgeon and philosopher in the Roman Empire, also described a medicine for the eyes made of Phrygian stone.[6] Aristotle spoke of it as a Phrygian powder. Professor and Sir W. M. Ramsay explains what kind of medicine it was by saying it was not an ointment but a cylindrical collyrium that could be powdered and then spread on the part affected.[7] The term used by John in Revelation, *kolluurion*,[8] is the same that Galen uses to describe the preparation, a diminutive form of the word for a "long roll of bread," of the Phrygian stone.[9]

Whether the water from Hierapolis cooled to lukewarm at Laodicea, or the cold water from Colossae merged with the hot water from Hierapolis, or the main source of water from the south arrived lukewarm, is not as important as is the main message to the church at Laodicea: "You are neither cold nor hot . . . You do not know that you are wretched, miserable, poor, blind, and naked . . . buy from Me gold refined in the fire that you may be rich . . . [wear] white garments [to hide your shame] and anoint your eyes with salve that you may see. . . [that you absolutely need the saving grace of the Lord Jesus] . . . be zealous and repent . . . I stand at the door

---

4. Gregg, *Revelation*, 114.

5. Johnson, *Revelation*, 456.

6. Ramsay, *Letters*, 419. Galen describes it as having the form of a tabloid made from the Phrygian stone, while Aristotle speaks of it as Phrygian powder; the two are probably identical.

7. Ramsay, *Letters*, 315.

8. Orr, "Eyesalve."

9. Padfield, *Colossae*, 6.

and knock, [open the door, answer my call] and sit with me on my throne" (Rev 3:15–21).

We live as a fallen creation and the past events and experiences of the seven churches are also precursors for today's churches as well as of the final judgment at the end of human history.

Section III—HEAVENLY VISIONS
and SEVEN JUDGMENT CYCLES
(Rev 4:1–21:8).

# Chapter Ten

# Cycle One

## The Scroll and Its Seven Seals (Rev 4:1–8:1)

IMAGERY IS ESPECIALLY IMPORTANT in apocalyptic literature. A trumpet sounded and Paul was caught up to heaven, whether in or out of body only God knows.[1] The scene of this vision is John in Heaven. Dispensationalists interpret this as the Rapture. I, and many others, do not. The claim is that in Rev 4:1–2, the rapture of the church is depicted. However, in this scene only John is taken to Heaven.

John sees a throne,[2] a control center of the universe, and five things stand out about the throne: what is on the throne, what comes from the throne, what is behind the throne, what is before the throne, and what is around the throne. God sat on the throne (Rev 4:2), an appearance like a jasper and a sardius stone. Perhaps John could not have been more descriptive of the One sitting on the throne beyond the inherent luminosity and brilliance of the precious stones because God's greatness and glory consistently exceed human comprehension. The main point is the marked contrast to Satan's throne referred to in the Pergamum church, Rev 2:13. Recall in Matt 17:5–6 when "a bright cloud overshadowed them; and suddenly a voice came out of the cloud, saying, 'This is My beloved Son, in whom I am well pleased. Hear Him!' And when the disciples heard it, they fell on their faces and were greatly afraid." Ezekiel also experienced a theophany of One on the throne, but some claim his vision was before the destruction

---

1. 2 Cor 12:2.

2. See Ezek 1 for the parallel throne vision.

of Jerusalem in 586 BCE by the Babylonians. The preterist might claim that John foresees the second destruction in AD 70, and the futurist might claim this as a significant turning point in the book of Revelation, as "after the church age." The main point is that Almighty God remains the control center of the universe and that Jesus "is the way, the truth, and the life. No one comes to the Father except through Me" (John 14:6).

Is the rainbow around the throne in 4:3 symbolic of the heavenly promise not to destroy the saints of God? Is this rainbow like the rainbow of God's earthly promise not to destroy the world by flood in Gen 9? Regarding the sound of the trumpet and John being caught up to heaven, I cannot help but think of the trumpet blast, the thundering, and the lightning in Exodus when Moses was called to Mount Sinai to receive the law. Exodus 24:10 records Moses and seventy elders seeing a visible manifestation of the Lord. There are other throne visions in the Old Testament. Micaiah, the son of Imlah, saw the Lord sitting on His throne and all the host of heaven standing by (1 Kgs 22:19). Ezekiel saw the glory of the Lord depart the city of Jerusalem and move east across the Kidron Valley to the Mount of Olives (Ezek 11:22–23). Daniel saw the Ancient of Days seated on His throne, a fiery flame (Dan 7:9). In Rev 4:2, John was called to heaven in the Spirit and received manifold revelation of God's absolute sovereignty and glory.

Surrounding the throne of God are twenty-four other thrones in which sat twenty-four elders (4:4). They are heavenly beings and form a picture of God surrounded by His people, a royal priesthood, the redeemed (1 Pet 2:9). Perhaps we should settle with such simple interpretation. After all, does it have to be more complicated? Do they represent the twelve patriarchs and the twelve apostles? Since angels are not called elders and do not wear white or gold crowns, the twenty-four elders may not be angels. However, these are the same elders, each having a harp and golden bowls full of incense, who fell before the Lamb in Rev 5:8. From among these elders, one asked John, "Who are these arrayed in white robes, and where did they come from?" (7:13). This elder answered his question with an explanation some identify as concerning the great tribulation (7:14–17). In this sense, the elders may be angelic interpreters. They are the same elders attending the voice of many waters, the harps, and the new song before the throne (14:3).

Embrace Ezekiel's vision of the Almighty in Ezek 8:2, recollect the reality that tribulations for Christians occur throughout the church age, and steer clear of any comparison to the about twenty-five men with their backs to the temple of the Lord (Ezek 8:16). Those were the men who devised iniquity and gave wicked counsel in the city. They were facing east, worshipping the sun, and were the corrupt priesthood of Ezekiel's day (Ezek 11:2). Recall that Ezekiel was exiled to Babylon nine years after Daniel. Ezekiel prophesied to the twelve tribes, warned against idolatry, and emphasized God's glory.

Also, around the throne are "four living creatures full of eyes in front and in back" (Rev 4:6b). Are these the same four creatures in the prophecies of Ezekiel and Daniel? In Ezek 1:5–11, the four living creatures had four faces and wings. John saw four creatures, each having six wings. Does the difference in the number of faces and wings matter? Is it a matter of perspective? For instance, the one stranded on an island rejoices at the sight of a boat and the one in the boat rejoices at the sight of land. Ezekiel and John saw one face like an ox (calf), another like a lion, another like a man, and one like an eagle. The four living creatures around the throne are magnificent angelic guardians with eyes to see everything and wings to get anywhere. The symbolic imagery represents their splendor beyond what human language can only hope to convey. In Ezek 10:14, one of the four faces was that of a cherub, different than the ox (calf) in the vision of Ezek 1:10. Differences matter.

The visions of Ezek 1 and John's vision in Rev chapter 4 are similar but distinct. Even Ezekiel's visions at the beginning of his book and those when glory departs from the temple in chapter 10 are distinct. The vision in Dan 7:3–8 is of four great beasts. One was like a lion, one was like a bear, one was like a leopard, and one was like no earthly animal. The patterns are similar, but it may be reckless for one to claim that the visions in Ezekiel and Daniel foreshadow or parallel the four creatures in Revelation.

The twenty-four elders are most likely heavenly beings with some authority since they are sitting around the throne. They are God's people, servants of The Almighty, and they have cast their crowns and fallen before the Lord in worship. They may be representative of, but they are not, the twelve tribes of Israel because they are not "sealed" until later in chapter 7. The twelve tribes and twelve apostles, indeed the number twelve, serve here only as a connectivity of the Old and New Testaments. Seven lamps of fire and the seven spirits of God were before the throne (Rev 4:5) along with a sea of glass-like crystal (4:6a). In 15:2, this sea of glass will be mingled with fire and occupied by the victorious. The sea of glass could represent several things, such as the waters of the red sea or the heavenly counterpart of the sea in Solomon's temple.

## God the King, and Christ the Worthy One (Rev 5)

With the image of God sitting on the throne still in John's mind, he sees God holding a sealed scroll with writing on the front and back. First-century Christians were no doubt familiar with the prophecy of the end times, written on a scroll presented in Dan 12:4. The scroll in Rev 5:1 might represent God's covenant, His law, His promises, His plans, or perhaps a legal will. "No one in heaven or on the earth or under the earth was able to open the scroll or look at it" (Rev 5:3). No wonder John wept. John had been whisked away in the Spirit, witnessing in wonderment events far removed from anything he had ever witnessed, and now he might be denied reading the clarifications. The scroll was written on the inside and the back and sealed with seven seals. The scroll in Ezek 2:9–10 was also written on the inside and the outside.

A slain Lamb, Jesus, who is worthy to take the scroll, takes it from God and opens the seals (Rev 5:9). Ezekiel gives a similar background, except he takes a scroll of a book with writing on the front and back and without seals from a "hand stretched out."[3] In the ancient world, scrolls were sealed with dollops of hot wax and then something authenticating, like a signet ring, was pressed into the seal for validation. Only the intended was authorized to break the seal and read the message.

When Jesus, the Lamb, took the scroll (5:8), praises began with the angels, then the elders, and then spread outward until the number of praises multiplied by ten thousand times ten thousand, and thousands of thousands. Hosts of redeemed humans, millions of angels, and other heavenly creatures are crying out before the throne and singing praises to God. This is corporate worship! Conceptually, the praises filled the universe.

Appearing as slain, the Lamb that took the scroll had seven horns and seven eyes. Horns symbolize strength (e.g., 2 Sam 22:3; Ps. 18:2), and the seven eyes are the seven Spirits of God sent out into all the earth, a metaphor for the fullness of the Holy Spirit. The critical point is that Jesus has apparent divine authority, is worthy to break the seals, and is the Spirit-empowered Messiah. Jesus is the agent through whom the God of the Universe's plan will come to pass. The Lion of the tribe of Judah and

3. See Ezek 2 and 3 regarding the opening and eating of the scroll.

the Worthy Lamb has overcome and reigns today and forever. John moves forward to fulfill Rev 1:19, "Write the things which you have seen, and the things which are, and the things which will take place after this."

Concluding cycle one is the first of a series of three judgment visions, each with seven elements: Seven seals (6:1–8:1); Seven trumpets (8:2–11:19); and Seven bowls (15:1–16:21). The seven trumpets will be addressed in Cycle Two, the seven symbolic histories will be addressed in Cycle Three (Rev 12–14), and the seven bowls will be addressed in Cycle Four. Like R. L. Dean, I assume a "telescopic interpretation of the three series of seven judgments each. That is, the seventh seal judgment includes and introduces the seven trumpet judgments, and the seventh trumpet judgment includes and introduces the seven bowl judgments."[4] This can also be understood as a sequential view where one judgment follows another. Revelation is prophesy. However, Revelation overall does not give us prophesy equated with prediction—it does not follow in a straight line. John is told to "Write the things which you have seen, and the things which are, and the things which will take place after this" (Rev 1:19). John's prophesies are things which he has seen, things which he sees, and things which will take place—many of which are yet unfulfilled. John's prophetic message is about Jesus and the people's faithfulness, or unfaithfulness, to Him. From the seven churches, John takes us back-and-forth to Heaven and Earth.

## *Opening Six Seals (Rev 6)*

On the scroll that Jesus, the Lamb, took are seven seals. Each seal represents a catastrophic event that is restrained (sealed). The opening of each seal releases a cause having severe consequences, and someone cries out or prays. Revelation 6 covers the six seals, but the seventh seal is not covered until Rev 8. The six seals are as follows:

> First Seal: The Conqueror
> Second Seal: Conflict on Earth
> Third Seal: Scarcity on Earth
> Fourth Seal: Widespread Death on Earth
> Fifth Seal: The Cry of the Martyrs
> Sixth Seal: Cosmic Disturbances

---

4. Dean "Chronological Issues," 218.

The vision of the breaking of the seals is cosmic, especially the first four because of John's use of the number four in four creatures, four horses, a fourth of the earth (Rev 6:8). "It is the number of the cosmos: four winds, four corners, etc."[5] The four creatures are calling for Jesus Christ the Lamb, and the four horsemen represent the kinds of things that happen[6] when the Kingdom of Jesus begin to press in on the world. Keep this in mind as you continue to read and remember the highly symbolic character of Revelation. Be careful about interpreting the imagery literally or even chronologically. A lamb with hooved feet could not grasp a scroll, and some events, like the timing of judgment, seem out of order. The seals are broken one at a time and all the seals must be broken before the scroll can be opened and read.

In the breaking of the first four seals, some contend that the activities of the four horsemen are only towards the Roman empire, and the blast of four of the seven trumpets are meant towards the entire earth but both could apply to past, present, and future. For example, we see the judgments associated with the seals, trumpets, and bowls threatened in Lev 26. In Leviticus, God describes the blessings that will come to Israel if she remains faithful to the covenant and the curses that will come if she is unfaithful. "And after all this, if you do not obey Me, then I will punish you seven times more for your sins" (Lev 26:18).

Regarding chronology, the visions John sees are presented in our Bible in a particular sequence, but that does not necessarily mean that all the judgments represented by the visions must occur in the same sequence. For instance, in chapter 11, following his vision of the seventh trumpet, John sees a vision symbolizing the birth of Christ (Rev 12:5), but the events involving the seventh trumpet did not precede the birth of Christ. However, a good argument can be made for a general sequence or succession in the judicial process in chapters 4–16. For example, after the seventh seal come the seven trumpets: "When He opened the seventh seal, there was silence in heaven for about half an hour. And I saw the seven angels who stand before God, and to them were given seven trumpets" (Rev 8:1–2). The main point is that the visions invite the audience to behold the full impact of God's sovereignty and triumphant reign through imaginative participation.

A sequential theological connection can be made when we consider the graduated intensity of the judgments. Compare the first seal, the white

5. Johnson, *Discipleship*, 169.
6. See Ezek 5 regarding the four plagues.

horse, to that of the fourth seal, Death and Hades are given power over a fourth of the earth (6:8). The increase continues after the seals when judgment surges from a fourth to a third in the following sequence with the first trumpet. "The first angel sounded: And hail and fire followed, mingled with blood, and they were thrown to the earth. And a third of the trees were burned up, and all green grass was burned up" (8:7). This rise in intensity impacts vegetation, marine life, freshwater, and heavenly bodies (8:9–12, 15). "Clearly, each series raises the crescendo of divine judgment to a higher pitch, and some form of sequence would best fit this framework."[7] Later, it is evident that sequence or succession of judgment is not as applicable in the seventh series and parallelism may be more appropriate. The thunder, noises, lightning, and an earthquake following the seventh seal (8:5) are parallel to the lightning, noises, thunder, earthquake, and great hail of the seventh trumpet (11:19) and the seventh bowl (16:18).

The first four seals represent the four horsemen. While there is no doubt about the nature of the second, third, and fourth rider, there is some debate about the identity and function of the first. The first is a white horse, appearing in the opening of the first seal as the conqueror, "and he went out conquering and to conquer" (Rev 6:2). Some say the rider is Jesus because later in Revelation, Jesus appears on a white horse, "Now I saw Heaven opened, and behold, a white horse. And He who sat on him was called Faithful and True, and in righteousness, He judges and makes war" (Rev 19:11). Can an argument be made that the rider on this first white horse in Rev 6 represents Jesus? Some reason that "conquest," as used in the rest of Revelation, is of demonic agents. However, "conquer" and "conquered" used throughout the rest of the Bible all denote actions to advance the Kingdom of God. Remember that the scroll might represent many things God wants to accomplish. The four horsemen are to deliver four of the seven things God has purposed.

Suppose we use the white horse depicted in Zech 1:8, 6:3, and 6:6 to support an argument that the first horseman having a bow and crown represents Christ, and the other three horsemen are responding to a divine invitation as bringers of disaster. After all, is not the rider on the white horse in Zechariah divine?

The four horsemen in Zechariah were commissioned to traverse the earth doing God's work: "These are the ones whom the Lord has sent to walk to and fro throughout the earth . . . We have walked to and fro

7. Davis, "Relationship between the Seals," 150.

throughout the earth, and behold, all the earth is resting quietly" (Zech 1:10–11). The four concealed horsemen in Zech 1:8 are the Lord's scouts and the four not-concealed chariots in Zech 6:3 and 6:8 are the four spirits of Heaven. However, the horsemen in Rev 6 represent conquest, war, famine, and death—hardly the work of the Lord unless the Lamb's activity is related to the disasters. The four living creatures fell before the Lamb and proclaimed the Lamb worthy of opening the seals (Rev 5:8–9). Could the vision demonstrate that the divine response to evil is not merely its eradication but its transformation into an instrument of God's purpose and power? The disasters are both imminent and realistic; they are conceivable based on evils that humans themselves can bring about and, as such, reveal how the future judgment of God can already be seen to operate in the current world order. God is not responsible for evil. Divine retribution for human sin in this passage is only partial, "power was given to them over a fourth of the earth" (Rev 6:8). There is a difference between the four horsemen in Zechariah and the four horsemen in Revelation. Differences matter.

Suppose we argue that the rider on this white horse represents an antichrist, a figure Irenaeus and many other readers claim to find in the book of Revelation but is mentioned as "antichrist" less than five times. Those are in First and Second John, not Revelation.[8] The Revelation Realist will focus on the living Christ and not the antichrist. The rider on the white horse has a bow but no arrow (no point in that). The rider is given only one crown instead of the many crowns Christ possesses in Rev 19:12. Suppose the rider on the first horse represents an antichrist (a false, deceptive messiah) and is imitating Christ's appearance and has no arrow. This counterfeit messiah is falsely alluding to peace through diplomacy. It is not certain the first horseman is an antichrist, but the rider is sure to be an agent of Satan. Satan is here to kill, steal, and destroy (John 10:10). Christ carries a two-edged sword throughout Scripture, not a bow, and a warrior with a bow and no arrow is a warrior "wannabe." Many commentaries claim the rider is an antichrist, and Rev 6–8 are judgments from God's throne. Christ is likely not the rider in the first seal. Still, Christ is indeed the rider in Rev 19:11, and the imagery in Rev 6 can have multiple applications throughout the church's history, including that, most probably, the rider is an antichrist. Remember, the four horsemen are to deliver four of the seven things God has purposed, and nothing in this world can occur apart from God's sovereign decree. War will characterize the period leading up to

8. Pagels, *Revelation*, 113.

Jesus's return, and this period will include an antichrist (1 John 2:18, 22, 4:3 and 2 John 1:7). Furthermore, the catastrophic events of the first four seals all belong to the same affair. Conflict follows conquest, which historically includes famine and widespread deaths.

The second horse is a fiery red horse and appears in the opening of the second seal to cause conflict on earth. Red is symbolic of blood and "it was granted to the one who sat on it to take peace from the earth, and that people should kill one another; and there was given to him a great sword" (Rev 6:4). The great sword (Gr. μαχαιρα) is one meant for violently butchering/slaying one another (Gr. αλληλους σφαξουσιν). The good and the wrong people will be slain with this sword. By God's providence, the second horseman can use the sword as an instrument of judgment, just as God used the Assyrians, the Babylonians, and the lions to refine and convert His kingdom. Evil generates war, and spiritual evil is the worst kind of evil. The period of the second horse is representative of the intensity of the Tribulation. With the first rider offering false peace, the second rider can use his sword to remove peace from the world. The preterist could use the prophecy in Matt 24:2, where Jesus predicts the temple's destruction, and the futurist could use prediction of the events in 24:6–8 where Jesus tells the disciples, "And you will hear of wars and rumors of wars. See that you are not troubled; for all these things must come to pass, but the end is not yet. For nation will rise against nation, and kingdom against kingdom. And there will be famines, pestilences, and earthquakes in various places. All these are the beginning of sorrows." The judgment is particular, the timing is uncertain, and such signs characterize the entire period between Christ's resurrection and Jesus's return in glory for judgment.

The third horse is black, appears in the opening of the third seal and the rider had a pair of scales or balances like one would use to measure and appropriate food and money, such as, "A quart of wheat for a denarius, and three quarts of barley for a denarius" (Rev 6:6). The color black and the scales each represent famine. Josephus reports terrible famine associated with the siege of Jerusalem by the Roman armies.[9] The scarcity on earth means greed and injustice, hunger, and starvation. Osborne writes, "A denarius was a day's wages, and a quart of wheat was sufficient daily food for one person. This means a man's daily wages could only feed himself, not his family."[10] Some might conclude that the rich are not affected because of the

9. Josephus, *Jewish Wars*, 429–30, 512–13.
10. Osborne, *Revelation Verse by Verse*, 86.

command to "not harm the oil and the wine"(6:6). However, I resolve that the oil and wine are representative of this, and other food supplies left unharmed. The oil and wine are quite possibly left for religious purpose. God tempers His judgment on the earth with grace, leaving some sustenance behind.

The fourth horse is pale grey, with Death as the rider and Hades following. "And power was given to them over a fourth of the earth, to kill with sword, with hunger, with death, and by the beasts of the earth" (Rev 6:8). Grey symbolizes death. The rider on the fourth horse brings death powerfully to a quarter of the earth. Death comes by the sword, famine, and even by beastly animals. We are not to think that exactly one-fourth of the population dies in God's judgment, but instead three-quarters survive. The judgment is measured. God is merciful.

The first four seals, the four horsemen, teach us that from the time Jesus Christ was on the throne, the disastrous functions of the four horsemen of the apocalypse have been trying to wipe us out by conquest, war, famine, and death. Then and now, and in the future, when we ignore or resist him and His way, the "four horsemen" will continue to ride. When violence is glorified and marketed, and millions are murdered through genocide and infanticide, the world will continue to suffer violence. God does not desire violence. The rise of violence is due directly to humanity resisting Jesus.

The four horsemen may represent the things that happen when Christ's Kingdom begins to press in on the world or when the world presses in on God's Kingdom. For reasons we do not yet fully comprehend, God intervenes by His divine prerogative and sovereignly places holy will into human hearts to do the things God wants them to do. God controls and directs them to fulfill the Almighty's purposes.[11] God will avenge the suffering of his people by bringing chaos and panic to the forces of evil in the cosmos. Divine judgment indiscriminately affects people regardless of their status. The four horsemen can be seen as underscoring the Roman world's vulnerability and God's judgment in the present world order. The disasters of old are replicated throughout history, and the tomorrow will likely join that history.

Regarding the fifth seal, The Cry of the Martyrs, John sees under "the altar all the souls of those who had been slain for the word of God and for the testimony which they held" (Rev 6:9).[12] Martyred saints cry out for justice,

---

11. Steven Lawson, *Foundations of Grace*, 501.

12. See Ezek 6 regarding the slain under the altar.

not for themselves but for God's justice to be fully manifested throughout the world. God is not responsible as an assailant for the martyred saints. Perhaps one of the closest representations of the fifth seal from Scripture is of the persistent widow wanting justice from her adversary, as told in Luke 18:1–8. As we yearn with the heavenly saints of God to pour out justice on the world, God reminds us of one thing: "rest a little while longer" (Rev 6:11). At this point in Revelation, we are not seeing what is happening on earth but rather what is happening in Heaven. "Shall God not avenge His elect who cry out day and night to Him, though He bears long with them?" (Luke 18:7). Throughout the rest of Revelation, John repeatedly attempts to address the martyrs' demand for divine justice.[13] The martyrs have paid the ultimate price and their relationship with Christ does not end in death.

Whether the martyrs' cry occurred in John's time, before or after the temple's destruction, is not principal to the story: cries for justice are heard today. The cries for justice are also the cries of injustice, and perhaps the cries of today should be replaced with measured anger against the atrocities of abortion, gun violence, and poverty. We are to be slow to anger. Unrestrained anger is sinful—injustice fuels righteous anger. Romans 12:19–21 tells us, "Beloved, do not avenge yourselves, but rather give place to wrath; for it is written, 'Vengeance is Mine, I will repay,' says the Lord. Therefore, if your enemy is hungry, feed him; if he is thirty, give him drink; for in so doing you will heap coals of fire on his head.' Do not be overcome by evil but overcome evil with good." We must be angered about worldly ways that are not God's ways. God is angered by unbelief, unfaithfulness, disobedience, crimes against divine laws, false God, sinful pride, and injustice, to name a few (Is 13:5; 51:20; Exod 15:7; 32:10–11; Num 11:1–2; 32:13; Job 4:9; Lam 2:2; Rom 2:5). We are to be careful to not confuse divine wrath with thine wrath. God is inexorably just; we are inescapably mortal.

Cosmic disturbance happens with the opening of the sixth seal. "There was a great earthquake; and the sun became black as sackcloth of hair, and the moon became like blood." (6:12). Stars and figs fall, the sky recedes, mountains and islands move, people hide in caves and wonder who can stand (6:13–17). These events appear to describe either a historical crisis or the second coming. However, Isaiah, Ezekiel, and Jeremiah all use such metaphorical language to describe the earlier judgments of Babylon, Egypt,

---

13. See Rev 8:3–5; 10:3–7; 11:1–2; 14:1–2; 14:1–3, 9–11, 13, 18; 15:1–4; 16:5–7; 18:8, 18, 20; 19:3.

and Judah. They, too, appear to describe the second coming.[14] Final judgment will not be reached until the "great supper of God" when those allied with the beast are defeated (13:16; 18:3) in a final eschatological battle (19:17–21).

The preterist might associate this with the temple's destruction in 70 CE. The futurist might associate all of this with the second coming of Christ. We must keep in mind that it could be neither. Contrast the judgments of Babylon in Isa 13 with the final destruction of the world in Isa 34:3–4. Notice the fall of Egypt in Ezek 30 and the 586 BCE destruction of the temple in Jerusalem in Ezek 33:21. Judgment and judgments occur without necessarily being the final judgment.

Does the opening of the sixth seal bring us to the edge of the final coming of the kingdom? Or is it only a first-century experience of the earthquake, blackened sun, blood moon, falling stars, figs, shifted mountains and islands, and men of all social status hiding in caves? Remember, prophesy in Revelation involves events in the present and the foretelling of events to come, just as in the Old Testament. For example, recall the fulfilled prophesies of Babylon, Nineveh, Tyre, and Edom. Think of the many OT prophesies about Jesus fulfilled in the New. In Revelation, the Spirit permits John to see events in the present and things that will happen (John sees Heaven). No other book of the Bible helps us see Jesus as Jesus is right now. Jesus is the same yesterday, today, and forever.

Therefore, the answer to the previous two questions is yes. The opening of the sixth seal (as other parts of Revelation) can be interpreted as having happened in the first century and being a foretelling of what is to come. Revelation seeks to set the present moment in light of the unseen realities of the future and the present. That is one reason why I do not dwell on any one of the hermeneutical approaches of futurist, historicist, preterist, idealist, or eclectic. From the six seals, we learn that sin is repugnant to God, the terrible intensity of the Tribulation, that God is concerned with injustices, left to themselves humans would never repent, and sinful people instinctively hide from God. This is one of the beauties of the Revelation about Jesus from Jesus. The Lord will undoubtedly judge all those who oppose Him. God chooses us, and if we decide not to follow, we stand in opposition.

14. See Babylon (Isa 13:1, 10, 19), Egypt (Ezek 32:2, 7–8, 16, 18), and Judah (Jer 4:14, 23–24).

## *Care for the Saints (Rev 7)*

Six of the seven seals were opened in Rev 6. However, some commentators tell us that the events at the beginning of Rev 7, The Sealed of Israel, occur before explaining the seals in Rev 6. They claim that the passage 7:1–8 is a fragment dislocated from its original context.[15] Perhaps they interpret the four winds in 7:1 as the four horsemen in 6:1–8. Zech 6:5 reads, "These are the four spirits [or winds] of heaven, who go out from their station before the Lord of all the earth." For now, it is easiest to see chapter 7 as an intermission with explanations between the chaos in Rev 6 and the chaos in Rev 8. The text is integrated with care into the narrative.

An angel ascending from the east tells the four angels commissioned to harm the earth and the sea to "not harm the earth, the sea, or the trees till we have sealed the servants of our God on their foreheads" (7:3). The faithful are sealed as a sign of protection and ownership.[16] The marks on the foreheads might also be related to where the law was placed as a symbol of loyalty to the Lord in Deut 11:18. The mark protected the faithful Israelites mourning the sins of Jerusalem before the six destroying angels were released in Ezek 9:4–6. In addition, Aaron wore a gold plate on the front of his turban. Engraved on this plate was: Holiness to the Lord. "It shall always be on his forehead, that they may be accepted before the Lord" (Exod 28:38).

The events in Rev 7 contrast with the destruction we just read about in chapter 6. There is a calm reflection before the seventh seal is opened in Rev 8 as 144,000 of all the tribes of the children of Israel are sealed. In Rev 7:9, the great multitude is clothed in white (purity) with palm branches in their hands (victory in war or celebrating the Feast of Tabernacles). One might say that the 144,000 represents a sea of humanity, perfection, or the fullness of twelve, multiplied by another fullness of twelve, multiplied by one thousand, which is a "completeness on steroids" or a number too large to count. The number cannot be taken with mathematical literalness if the number is symbolic.

The "seal of the living God" is sometimes associated with the rite of Baptism. Chapter 7 answers the Rev 6:17 question, "Who is able to stand?" Revelation 7:1 should not be regarded as a chronological marker because what is written about the four angels is also told in Rev 6:1–8. It is not

15. Bousset, *Die Offenbarung Johannis,* 283–84.

16. See Ezek 9:4.

a fragment dislocated from its original content but rather a script incorporated with precision into the story. At the beginning of Rev 7, the four angels, four corners (representing all the earth), and the four winds take us back to the four seals and the four horsemen of Rev 6.[17]

John hears the number of those sealed is 144,000, which is all the tribes of the children of Israel (Rev 7:4). Jacob had twelve sons, and he gave his son Joseph a double portion. This meant that each of his sons, Ephraim, and Manasseh, became a tribe rather than just the one tribe of Joseph (Gen 48:5). It is essential to recognize the twelve tribes listed in Rev 7 are the tribes of Israel. However, they do not correspond to the twelve tribes in Gen 29–30, Num 1, or Deut 27:12–13. John begins the list in Revelation with Judah first instead of Rueben, but more significant is that John omits the tribe of Dan. The omission of the tribe of Dan is likely due to the tribe's association with idolatry, referenced in Judg 18:30–31 and 1 Kgs 12:28–30. The tribe of Ephraim is also missing but is replaced with Ephraim's father, Joseph. The tribe of Dan is replaced with the tribe of Levi, and the number of tribes remains at twelve. The main point is that genealogical lists in the Bible are significant, and differences infer a theological statement, a statement not explained by John. The exactness of 144,000 indicates that the sealed are fully accounted for and known.

After seeing the 144,000, John sees a "great multitude which no one could number" (Rev 7:9). This is a Hebrew way of saying it is a big, big, number. This also shows the fulfillment of God's promise to Abraham of innumerable descendants (Gen 22:17; Gal 3:29). The announcement of the seventh seal is delayed while the fullness of God's people (the twelve Jewish tribes of Israel), and the Gentiles (included in the great multitude of all nations) are sealed. Ephesians 4:30 tells us that gentile believers are also sealed, and this is further emphasized in the great multitude narrative of Rev 7:14–17. Some commentators claim that the number includes only Jewish believers.[18] However, the children of God are determined not by ethnic heritage but by faith.

17. See Ezek 7 regarding the wrath of God.

18. The "servants of our God" must also include Gentiles on equal status with the Jews, as Paul tells us in Eph 2:11–22. In addition, God gave no inheritance in Israel to the tribe of Levi (Josh 13:14), and the tribes of Ephraim and Dan are excluded from the 144,000 (Dan was excluded perhaps because of their earlier association with idolatry (Judg 18). Worth noting is that Abraham, Isaac, and Jacob were not from any of the tribes of Israel.

We learn a few things from the catastrophes when the sixth seal is opened, which bears repeating. Sin is repugnant to God. Jesus washed us from our sins in his blood. (Rev 1:5). Throughout history, Christians will experience tribulation. Many who make it through the tribulation will have the purity of white robes washed in the blood of the Lamb. (Rev 7:14). God is concerned with injustices. Jesus declares justice to the Gentiles (Matt 12:18). Humans left to themselves will never repent. "But the natural man does not receive the things of the Spirit of God, for they are foolishness to him; nor can he know them, because they are spiritually discerned" (1 Cor 2:14). Sinful people instinctively hide from God. "Fall on us and hide us from the face of Him who sits on the throne and from the wrath of the Lamb!" (Rev 6:16).

Another Hebrew way, or at least in Jewish literature at that time, is for one to ask a question of which the answer is already known.[19] In Rev 7:13 one of the elders asked John, "Who are these arrayed in white robes and where did they come from?" The elder then proceeds to identify the multitude as those who have been through great tribulation, who no longer hunger or thirst, and who have washed their clothes white in the blood of the lamb. In other words, these are the believers of every tongue and tribe and their suffering for the sake of Christ is not overlooked. The sealed are protected from God's wrath and from the ultimate consequences—the pouring out of the seven bowls which will be explained in Rev 8–16.[20]

### *Opening the Seventh Seal (Rev 8:1)*

No seals were opened in Rev 7, and some commentators regard that chapter as an interlude before the seventh seal is opened in Rev 8. The content of the sixth seal begins in Rev 6:12 and brings cosmic catastrophe. Could this be an answer to the martyr's request for judgment from when the fifth seal was opened in Rev 6:9–11? However, judgment cannot yet occur because Rev 7:3 is written, "Do not harm the earth, the sea, or the trees till we have sealed the servants of God on their foreheads." Therefore, Rev 7:3 must be

---

19. Of course, this practice is without expiration.

20. "The hundred and forty-four thousand who were redeemed from the earth. 4 These are the ones who were not defiled with women, for they are virgins. These are the ones who follow the Lamb wherever He goes. These were redeemed from *among* men, *being* first fruits to God and to the Lamb. 5 And in their mouth was found no deceit, for they are without fault before the throne of God" (Rev 14:3–5).

a pericope of Rev 6. The sixth seal and Rev 7 finish with an eschatological-like conclusion like what is seen in Rev 21 and 22.

In Rev 7:13, an elder answers his question to John about the ones arrayed in white robes. The only other time in Revelation where an elder explains to John is when John wept about the sealed scroll in 5:4–5. In some regard, the two passages of elder responses might form an inclusio or a bracketed, framed structure. The elder dialog about the scroll and the seven seals are introduced at the beginning, before the seals, and the elder dialog in Rev 7 serves to constitute a complete narrative cycle. The seventh seal is subsequently opened, and there is silence.

In Rev 8, the seventh seal, Prelude to the Seven Trumpets, is opened, and "there was silence in Heaven for about half an hour" (Rev 8:1). Half an hour equates to a moment of time. But circumstances weigh heavily upon a moment of time. The moments of time passing while a person is drowning cannot be equated with the same amount of time sunning on a beach. Every instant of delay expands into hours or even ages. The anticipation of what is to come in this half an hour during these series of judgments was likely agonizing. Heaven stands in awe of the presence of Christ and the prospect of what is to occur. All heaven becomes mute and breathless. God does not require silence in Heaven to hear the prayers of Saints who are, along with the angels, quiet while waiting for the results of the seventh seal opened. The silence is not explained. One possible explanation might be as an application for self-reflection. At what periods in your life do you fall silent for half an hour? Another cause could be one of expectation. The multitude in Heaven stands in awe of what is about to happen and eagerly awaits in silence.

Seven angels are given seven trumpets.[21] Author D.W. Johnson writes a very expressive statement, "The images need to be heard in order to be seen."[22] John writes that those who read and hear the words are blessed. However, the content of the seventh seal is not read but visually and audibly revealed after this period of silence. Before the first trumpet, another angel, not one of the seven, holds a golden censer with incense and the saints' prayers ascend to God.[23] The angel fills it with fire, tosses it to earth, and causes noise, thunder, lightning, and earthquake (Rev 8:5). A censer of gold

---

21. In the book of Tobit, Raphael announces himself as one of the seven angels (Rev 12:15), and chapter 20 of the book of Enoch lists the names of the seven angels.

22. Johnson, *Discipleship*, 191.

23. Paul speaks of the golden censer as belonging to the tabernacle (Heb 9:4).

is an implement belonging to the Holy of holies. In Luke 12:49, Christ says, "I came to send fire on the earth." Could this "another angel" be Jesus, the Son of God? There are references to "another angel" in Revelation with little support in the narrative to conclude that "another angel" is Jesus. In Rev 14, four instances of "another angel" join "One like the Son of Man." The "another angel" is undoubted of a superior order. Compare this judgment unleashed by the first trumpet to when the Lord told Moses to stretch out his hand, and hail, thunder, and fire followed (Exod 9:22–25). Regardless of who this priestly angel is, John introduces the more important point: signs of punishment—noises, thundering, lightning, and an earthquake, which cover the earth.

The seven trumpets are to warn the world of the pending judgment. Recall from the Old Testament that trumpets announce the presence of the Lord at Mt. Sinai (Exod 19:16) and when the Israelites gathered for the feasts (Num 10:10). Trumpets also announce the coming of God to defeat enemies in Josh 6 and Joel 2:1–11. Trumpets connect with war (Num 10:9; Jer 4:19). Trumpets were used to call the congregation and for directing the movement of the camps (Num 10:2). Trumpets were used to announce royalty (1 Kgs 1:34, 39; 2 Kgs 9:13). Trumpets were used in the overthrow of the ungodly and in bringing down of the walls of Jericho (Josh 6:13–16). Furthermore, even with all the devastation, judgment is not total but fractional—one-third fractional, in fact, but again the mathematics is not to be taken literally. God is merciful, shows restraint, and is always just and true.

# Chapter Eleven

# Cycle Two

## Seven Angels with Seven Trumpets (Rev 8:2–11:19).

FOUR OF THE SEVEN trumpets of judgment compare with the plagues against the unbelieving Egyptians but in favor of the believing Hebrews during the exodus. The seven trumpets are associated primarily with the judgment of Jerusalem. Like Egypt, Israel will be judged with similar irruptions.

### *Seven Angels before God (Rev 8:2–6)*

The trumpets set into motion seven judgments. The first four trumpets are directed towards nature and the last three towards humanity. Each of the sounding seven trumpets devastate something, and for an important reason only the first four are covered in Rev 8.

> First trumpet—vegetation
> Second trumpet—seas
> Third trumpet—waters
> Fourth trumpet—heavens

The description of the devastation caused by the sounding of the first four trumpets is concise. Just as the judgments of the first four horsemen, these judgments are executed according to God's plan. The description of the devastation caused by the sounding of the fifth and sixth trumpets is protracted in Rev 9, and just as between the opening of the sixth and seventh seals, there is an interlude between the sixth and seventh trumpets. We read about the effects of the seventh trumpet in Rev 11:15.

Claiming with certainty that a particular Scripture describes how the endtimes will appear places our way above God's way and is a blatant expression of unbelief, impatience, and arrogance. The phenomena of thunder, lightning, and earthquake described in Rev 8:5; 11:19; and 16:18–21 do not imply the end of history any more than the manifestation of storm and fire described in Exod 19:16 implied the end of history.[1] However, we are never wrong to speak of the might of God's awesome acts and declare His greatness (Ps 145:6).

## *Six Angels Blow Their Trumpets (Rev 8:7–9:21)*

The first trumpet brings hail and fire and destroys only a third of the trees but all the green grass. [2] The second trumpet put *something like* a burning green mountain into the sea, a third of which became blood where a third of the creatures died, and a third of the ships were destroyed.[3] If the first trumpet damaged the environment, commerce is weakened in the advent of the second trumpet. The loss of agriculture, marine life, and maritime conveyance directly impacts physical nourishment. We see graduated judgment from the seals to the trumpet's partial effect to the bowl's total effect. The third trumpet caused a star named Wormwood to fall through the midst of Heaven and poison the rivers and springs, killing many men who drank of the water (Rev 8:11).[4]

---

1. Mathison, *From Age to Age*, 671.

2. "And Moses stretched out his rod toward heaven; and the Lord sent thunder and hail, and fire darted to the ground. And the Lord rained hail on the land of Egypt. So there was hail, and fire mingled with the hail, so very heavy that there was none like it in all the land of Egypt since it became a nation" (Exod 9:23–24). See Ezek 5:1–4 and 12 about the one-third destruction.

3. Exod 7:14–24: "19 Then the Lord spoke to Moses, 'Say to Aaron, "Take your rod and stretch out your hand over the waters of Egypt, over their streams, over their rivers, over their ponds, and over all their pools of water, that they may become blood."'"

4. Wormwood, a member of the Asteraceae family, is an herb (a herb in Britain), and its most notable plant compound is thujone, which has some benefits but can be toxic in excess. Wormwood grows readily across various climates. Bener, "Modeling and Optimizing," 358.

The fourth trumpet causes a third of the sun, the moon, and the stars to darken, affecting day and night. This is like the prophetic descriptions of the day of the Lord in Amos 5:20, "Is not the day of the Lord darkness, and not light? Is it not very dark, with no brightness in it?" And Zeph 1:15, "That day is a day of wrath, A day of trouble and distress, A day of devastation and desolation, A day of darkness and gloominess, A day of clouds and thick darkness." Again, Revelation alludes to or echoes Old Testament texts.

The fifth trumpet is preceded by the "angel flying through the midst of Heaven" from where Wormwood fell. This angel is warning the inhabitants of the earth with a "woe, woe, woe" about the havoc coming when the following three trumpets sound (Rev 8:13).[5] Perhaps that is why there are three woes, one for each of the following three trumpets. John does not see the star fall when the fifth angel sounded the fifth trumpet. Still, he saw that a star *had* fallen, and to this star was given the key to the bottomless pit or shaft to the abyss (9:1). The star is Satan, not a real star, and a bottomless pit is simply a shaft running through a spool of thread or a tunnel through a mountain. Is the pit without a bottom? Is the abyss not the bottom? When the angel opens the pit, smoke rises from the abyss and darkens the sun and the air (cf. Luke 10:18).

The angel of the bottomless pit, Satan, unleashes a demonic army of locusts empowered as scorpions to bring five months of torment to everyone except those who are sealed, the believers.[6] They were told not to harm the trees or green things. The locusts are figurative: they do not eat grass or any green thing. For a locust to not eat anything green is a locust without purpose. However, these crowned locusts with man-like faces are supernatural and horse-shaped. They are equipped with breastplates, hair like a woman, teeth like a lion, and wings that sound like horse-drawn chariots running into battle. A locust with a stinger and a scorpion's abilities symbolizes harmful tribulation. Is it smoke coming from the pit, or are the locusts so thick that the collective appears as smoke? The locusts were not given authority to kill believers but to torment those without the seal

5. For "angel," some biblical versions use the Greek word *aetos* (eagle), and others use *angelos* (messenger/angel). Does it matter? Something was flying around, delivering God's warning.

6. Commentaries must be read with the same caution as any other interpretive literature. One commentary claimed a correlation between this five-month plague and the life expectancy of the locust when in fact, the life cycle of the locust is closer to 5 to 10 weeks and not about five months. It is not about the lifecycle of the locust.

of God on their foreheads for five months. Interestingly, and according to author F. F. Bruce, the Roman siege of Jerusalem lasted about five months.[7]

Ironically, the Greek name of this angel of the bottomless pit is Apollyon, which may be an allusion to Nero or Domitian, both of whom saw themselves as like Apollo. The armies in Judg 6:5 and 7:12 are compared to locusts, and John may be using the depiction of the locusts analogous to the Roman armies of Vespasian and Titus. The vision of locusts with scorpion tails depicts the self-defeating and tormenting nature of demonic wickedness that affects the human soul. The first woe is past.

From the four horns of the golden altar, John hears a voice telling the sixth angel to "Release the four angels who are bound at the great river Euphrates" (Rev 9:13). The four corners of the altar are called "horns." The Aramaic word for horn is *qeren,* and there are at least six different uses of the word horn. In Hebrew, the spelling is the same for each, and only the reading of the word in context differentiates whether the horn is musical, a corner, a ray, of strength, a hill, or a flask.[8] Many illustrations of the golden altar depict actual goat or ram horns protruding from the corners of the altar, but that is a misrepresentation for the altar in Rev 9:13, and possibly for the altar in Exod 37:25 where its horns were of one piece with the altar of incense.

The sixth trumpet unleashes four angels and ushers in an army of horsemen. The four angels were released from the river Euphrates at a predetermined time to kill a third of mankind. Recall that the fourth seal judgment of Rev 6:8 reduced the population by one-fourth. In Rev 7:2, the four angels are told not to harm. The four angels in Rev 9:15 are released to kill, further reducing the population by one-third, equating to exactly one-half the original population being destroyed.[9] Sovereign God is in control of the timed release of these four angels to the hour and day and month and year. These four agents of destruction were released seemingly without any conditional delay.

In contrast, the four angels in Rev 7:3 are restrained from harming the earth, the sea, and the trees until the faithful are sealed. Could they be the same four destructive angels? According to Simon Peter, a bondservant

---

7. Bruce, *New Testament History,* 382, as quoted by Mathison in *From Age to Age,* 673.

8. Similarly, the English word "light" can refer to illumination, something not heavy, dark, or ignite.

9. The original population (100) reduced by one-fourth (25) equals 75. Seventy-five reduced by one-third is 75 minus 25, which equals 50, or half the population.

and apostle of Jesus Christ, "God did not spare the angels who sinned, but cast them down to hell and delivered them into chains of darkness, to be reserved for judgment" (2 Pet 2:4). Most English versions of the Bible insert the word "hell" in place of *Tartarus,* the Greek word Peter used in that verse. Tartarus is the deepest and most distinct of subterranean places of all. Hill implies that Tartarus is the abode of fallen angels.[10] Christfried writes that Tartarus "marks the greatest distance from the heavenly world."[11] The Lord knows how to reserve the unjust under punishment for the day of judgment (2 Pet 2:9).

Hell is different from hades in that the punishment in Hell is not for a moment temporary, and Hades is where, since Christs' resurrection, the wicked await their ultimate ruin. The best example of the difference between Hell and Hades is the parable of Dives and Lazarus in Luke 16:19–31, where the rich man, not physically dead but tormented, sees and communicates perhaps moments before death. Regarding the manner of Hades, there is a difference between the Old and New Testaments.

In the Old Testament, the word used to describe the realm of the dead is Sheol, "Will they go down to the gates of Sheol? Shall we have rest together in the dust?" (Job 17:16). Hades is used in the New Testament to describe the realm of the tormented. Quoting King David writing about Jesus, Luke records, "For You will not leave my soul in Hades, Nor will You allow Your Holy One to see corruption" (Acts 2:27).

Did Christ descend to Hell as indicated in the Apostle's Creed? Debatable. On the cross, Jesus experienced the familiar lot of man in that he truly came to know what it means to die. He took on a human nature in the lowest regions of the earth. Jesus took the form of a bondservant (Phil 2:7). Of the texts most often used to support Christ's descending (Acts 2:27; Rom 10:6–7; Eph 4:8–9; and 1 Pet 4:6.13) 1 Pet 3:18–20 is the "strongest-of-the-weakest" and is the most confusing. Grudem considers the "troublesome phrase 'he descended into hell' a late intruder into the Apostles' Creed that really never belonged there in the first place and that, on historical and Scriptural grounds, deserves to be removed."[12]

Williams writes, "Martin Bucer and Theodore Beza rejected the idea of a literal descent, and on the basis of the biblical connection between hades and the grave both men thought of the descensus as a mere repetition

10. Hill, "Hades of Hippolytus," 115.

11. Böttrich, "Angel of Tartarus," 515.

12. Grudem, "He Did Not Descend," 103.

of 'died and was buried.'"[13] Additionally, other Reformers could find no biblical warrant for such an interpretation of the Creed.

The four angels in Rev 9:15 are released to kill. Just as it is possible for the blind to sense the presence of many people in a room, John could hear the number of horsemen of unequaled magnitude, which he determined to be two hundred million.[14] Symbolically, this is the largest military operation in history. It is also greater than the population of the entire Mediterranean world when John is writing. The four angels were bound at the Euphrates River. While it is the longest river in southwest Asia, rising in Turkey and flowing southwest across Syria and through Iraq, it is considered "north" relative to Israel. Most invasions came from that direction.[15] John's Roman audience feared an invasion from the Patheon Empire coming from the east. The Euphrates separated the promised land from the Roman Empire. The Assyrians crossed the Euphrates to carry Israel into captivity, and the Babylonians crossed the Euphrates to take Judah into captivity.[16]

John hears the number of the army and then sees the horses in his vision. The invasion was horrifying, with horses having heads like lion's heads, breathing out fire, smoke, and sulfur, and wounding with their serpent-like tails. Yet the survivors of the plagues of fire, smoke, and brimstone (sulfur) did not repent of their wicked ways of demonic worship, sexual immorality, and materialism. These judgments do not result in repentance. Like Pharaoh in the time of Moses, their hearts were hardened, and they continued to engage in evil. "And they did not repent of their murders or their sorceries or their sexual immorality or their thefts" (Rev 9:21). Such is the case, as we continue to learn throughout human history. Jesus says it is not simply the one who decides to follow but rather, "For whoever does the will of My Father in heaven is My brother and sister and mother" (Matt 12:50).

It is worth taking a pause here to reflect upon something I mentioned in the preface regarding the historicist, the preterist, the futurist, and the idealist. The historicist might interpret the vision of the locusts as a depiction of the Islamic conquest in a degenerate Western Europe (612–762 CE), or perhaps the two hundred million horsemen were Turks and Tartars using

13. Williams, "He Descended into Hell?," 84.

14. Some versions read, "twice ten thousand times ten thousand," which is the same number, two hundred million, but in antiquity, "two hundred million" did not exist.

15. Fee, *Revelation*, 134.

16. Gregg, *Revelation*, 236.

their great guns (fire, smoke, and brimstone) at the siege of Constantinople. The preterist might view the vision of the locusts as the invasion of the Roman armies leading to the destruction of Jerusalem or fulfillment of Deut 28, where Moses warned Israel that violating their covenantal relationship with God would scatter them among all peoples. Futurists might understand the vision as a supernatural plague of demonic spirits to be loosed on the earth shortly before the second coming. The idealist might depict the sounding of the trumpets vision as the self-defeating and tormenting nature of demonic wickedness that affects the human soul. Powers from the abyss attack only the wicked. None of these views can stand independently. All the visions and interpretations can have multiple applications for the past, present, and future. The realist understands that Almighty God can use all things to accomplish God's plan. That is the splendor of Revelation.

## *Care for John and the Two Witnesses (Rev 10:1–11:14)*

John sees another mighty angel coming down from Heaven, wrapped in a cloud. Just as there was an interlude between seals six and seven, a series of events occur between trumpets six and seven, and the second woe is yet to come. John is cared for by an angel, and the two witnesses could be Moses and Elijah or a historical allusion to the two high priests, Ananas and Joshua. But there is much more to unpack in this part of Revelation. It seems God is delaying judgment, and we are held in suspense before the seventh angel blows his trumpet. An angel tells John not to write about what the seven thunders have uttered and that there should be "delay no longer" (Rev 10:6). We are reminded that we do not get to know all the mysteries of God. To us, there is delay but God is not constrained by time and space. Since the life, death, resurrection, and ascension of Christ, we have been in the last days. As Peter tells us in Acts 2, we live in the final part of history, the era between the redemption accomplished in Jesus and the consummation of Christ's return.

Let's begin Rev 10 with some discussion about the angels delivering the messages. Contrast the angel in Rev 7:2 and the angel in 8:3 with the angel in 10:1. The "another mighty angel" in 10:1 is clothed with a cloud, the symbol of majesty. This angel has a rainbow of peace upon his head, and the face intensely bright like the sun, upon which is so bright one cannot look. This angel also has feet like pillars of fire, unlike eyes like a flame of fire or feet like fine brass as the Son of God in Rev 2:18. Standing with his right foot on the sea and his left foot on the land, one might think this angel is Jehovah God. However, the work to be accomplished by this angel required the interposition of one of higher order than the other heavenly inhabitants. If this angel is not Christ, the angel is undoubtedly a symbol of Divine majesty.

Is the Angel in Rev 10:5 Jesus Christ? The vision of the mighty Angel may be just short of a Christophany, a visual representation of Christ, an angel with divine authority. This Angel is different than the sixth messenger Angel in Rev 9:13 and the messenger angel who sounds the seventh trumpet in Rev 11:15. The mighty angel may be the same as when John is first commissioned: "He sent and signified it by His angel to His servant John" (Rev 1:1), and perhaps is the strong angel who proclaimed with a loud voice: "Who is worthy to open the scroll and loose its seals?" (Rev 5:2). Not all angels are a theophany, a visual representation of God, or a Christophany, a visual representation of Christ. The angel of God in Gen 21:17 is clearly distinguished in context from the Angel of the Lord, a theophany, in Gen 16:9.

The mighty angel coming down from Heaven in Rev 10:1 is likely not a Christophany (Christ is not an angel). John does not worship this angel as he worshiped Christ in Rev 1:17. Furthermore, there is no evidence that Christ comes to earth midway through the tribulation. This angel "swore by him who lives forever and ever" (Rev 10:6). This angel is Christophany-like by appearing clothed with a cloud which symbolizes the presence of God as in Exod 16:10. This angel is crowned with a rainbow as in "a rainbow around the throne, in appearance like an emerald" (Rev 4:3).[17] His face was like the sun (covered in glory) and feet like pillars of fire much like "His feet were like fine brass, as if refined in a furnace" (Rev 1:15). This angel's magnificence reinforces the power and deific source of the message. The important points are that Christ is communicating through an angel in this passage, there is nothing to hinder Christs' appearance as an angel, and the nature of the messenger must be determined by the context.

John is cared for by the angel who gives him the little book, which was "open in the hand of the angel who stands on the sea and, on the earth" (Rev 10:8), the same majestic angel who may be Christophany. The angel tells John to eat the book.[18] This is symbolic, of course, and Jeremiah provided

17. The details of God's appearance in Rev 4:3 is not described, reminding us that His greatness and glory always exceed human comprehension.

18. See Ezek 2:8, "open your mouth and eat what I give you."

a reference for us in Jer 15:16, where he too "ate the words of God" as did the prophet Ezekiel when he was commissioned as a prophet (Ezek 3:1–2). John finds God's word sweet as honey then turned bitter to "prophesy again about many peoples, nations, tongues, and kings" (Rev 7:9; 10:11; 11:9; and 17:15). This bittersweetness is the effect of suffering followed by victory.[19] Sweet is the Word of God, and bitter is the prophecy of trials and tribulation; suffering and perseverance needed to endure. The content of the book contains "lamentations and mourning and woe" (Ezek 2:10).

Is the "little" scroll given to John in Rev 10 the same scroll introduced in Rev 5? John has been proclaiming truths associated with the first scroll, and he eats the opened little scroll to proclaim more truths. It may be the same scroll. According to Joseph A. Seiss, both documents were small rolls and are diminutives of βιβλος—different forms of the same word.[20] The implication is that the words John is about to use are directly from God. The scroll is the Word of God, and once eaten, John speaks the words of God. The description of "little" does not differentiate the scrolls. The lesson is that we can "eat the word" of God and find its bitter-sweet implications. Truth is divine. "Truth is an out-of-this-world entity. It comes down from another realm. It comes from the character and mind of God himself."[21] That is the scroll's content. The angel who before addresses John continues to address John in the next sequence of events.

In Rev 11, John is told to measure the temple of God, the altar, and those who worship there. Is John being told to measure the temple in Jerusalem before it was destroyed in 70 CE? How can John measure the worshippers? The temple was destroyed in 70 CE by the Romans; thus, with a later date approach, the measurement of the temple must be symbolic.[22] With an early date approach, before the destruction of the temple, it must also be symbolic since John is to measure the worshippers as well. A handful of accounts claim this chapter is the most difficult to interpret in all of Revelation. The difficulty seems to hinge on whether we are to read the narrative of chapter 11 symbolically or literally. No rational person would enter a strictly literal interpretation of Revelation, yet a symbolic interpretation exclusive of any literal takeaways will restrict a fuller understanding.

---

19. See Ezek 25–32 for proclamations against nations.

20. Seiss, *Apocalypse*, 227.

21. Lawson, *Moment of Truth*, 9–10.

22. See Ezek 40–43 regarding measuring the temple.

John moves from being a seer to a worker. John is given a reed-like measuring rod and a task to measure the temple, much like the man in the scene played out in Ezek 40. The striking difference is between the literal and the symbolic. The story in Ezekiel comprehensively moves from the literal to symbolic, whereas the movements of John must first be recognized symbolically because the temple has long since been destroyed by the Romans, given a later-date approach to Revelation. There is simply no physical temple to measure. In fact, every notion of the temple or a temple throughout Revelation can be viewed symbolically. God's people are the temple. The church, the mystic temple, the spiritual house, is the temple. Since the destruction in 70 CE and the human manifestation of Christ, the believers have become the temple of God.

John is being told to measure the dimensions and boundaries of all God is appropriating. Note that this task is not visionary. It is not a vision of John or someone taking measurements but a command to measure the temple, the altar, and the worshipers. In much the same way as man measures to take possession, God is having measured the settlement of some new order. Notice that from this point in Rev 11, it is about what *will* happen and not what *is* or *did* happen. The man in Ezek 40 made actual measurements of the temple, but John is tasked with essentially "measuring" the presence of God on earth with His people. The altar and those who worship there represent the true worshipers of God, who are sealed and protected (see Rev 7). The angel tells John not to bother measuring outside the temple, explaining that the outer portion has been given to the Gentiles who "will tread the holy city underfoot for forty-two months" (Rev 11:2). The verses in Rev 11 may be more figurative of preserving God's people during attacks. The temple may symbolize the true church or the temple that will be rebuilt prior to the second coming of Christ, or the measurement itself is simply symbolic of God's ownership and protection (see Ezek 40:3; Zech 2:1–5).

The same angel who gives John the measuring rod can give specific miraculous powers to two witnesses. The witnesses will prophesy for one thousand two hundred and sixty days (forty-two months, thirty days each). They are clothed in sackcloth which may represent prophets.[23] They can offer repentance; the fire proceeding from their mouth can devour their enemies; they can stop the rain, turn water into blood, and strike earth with

---

23. Isaiah may have always worn sackcloth (Isa 20:2).

all plagues.[24] No other prophets have ever been given this much power. Even though the angel presents them as the two olive trees and lampstands, they are most likely actual persons. They stand before the God of the earth. When they finish their testimony, they will be killed by the beast and their bodies will lay in the street for three and a half days (Rev 11:7).[25] Zechariah had a vision of two olive trees where one was Zerubbabel, the governor of Judaea, and one was Joshua the high priest (Zech 4). According to Josephus, anti-zealots Ananas and Joshua were murdered in Jerusalem and left unburied. Although it appears more likely the witnesses were historic persons rather than symbolic of the church, there is not enough evidence to identify them with certainty. Tony Siew writes that the two witnesses are "prophets in mourning for the fate of Jerusalem and God's holy temple in the time of great tribulation lasting for three-and-a-half years until the kingdom of God Comes (11:15)."[26] Some commentaries show the lampstands as symbolic representations once used in the actual temple and the olive trees as symbolic representations of the source of the oil used in the lampstands. Recall that Rev 1:20 says that lampstands represent churches. The oil keeps the lamp lit, God's light shining. The prophet-witnesses apparently expose sin and bring some to repent. Other commentaries claim the witnesses are not actual people but are symbolic of the Christian church and of Israel. It is difficult to conceive of this symbolism standing before the Lord, clothed in sackcloth, killed, laying in the street for three and a half days, burial denied, the breath of God entering them, and them hearing a loud voice from Heaven.

The witnesses could be Moses and Elijah. Moses and Elijah appeared on the Mount of transfiguration with Jesus. Their power is represented in Exod 7:17–20; 1 Kgs 17:1; 2 Kgs 1:10; and Jer 5:14. Moses brought water from a rock, changed his staff into a snake, and parted the Red Sea. Elijah called down fire from Heaven and stopped the rain for three and a half years. Perhaps Moses represents the law, and Elijah represents the prophets, ending the Old Testament Jewish covenant with God and beginning the New Covenant with all nations as the children of God. Some claim the witnesses are Enoch and Elijah. After Jesus' transfiguration on the Mount, "His

24. Can the withholding of the rain be taken as God's word withheld as in Deut 32:2 and Isa 55:10?

25. The parallel verse about the two lampstands is in Dan 12:7.

26. Siew, *War Between the Two Beasts*, 217.

disciples asked Him, saying, 'Why then do the scribes say that Elijah must come first?'"(Matt 17:10).

Seiss asserts that the apocryphal Gospels are "very positive and clear in the assertion, that Enoch, with Elijah, is to witness again upon the earth."[27] He also draws support for the implication of these two witnesses from the Gospel of Nicodemus. While this early church literature is not widely recognized as doctrine, it must be recognized as current among Christians when they were written. However, more importantly, it should remind the reader of Revelation to focus only on the Sacred Word and the inspiration of the Holy Spirit against stilted theories and rationalistic systems of men. Otherwise, the possible interpretations are endless. After all, Paul was likely aware of the tradition in the early Jewish account of The Life of Adam and Eve and other non-canonical writings. The inerrancy of Scripture defines the authority of the Bible. God cannot tell a lie, and Holy Scripture reveals his God-breathed truth; therefore, Scripture is inerrant, and the authority of Scripture is inescapably impaired if this total divine inerrancy is in any way limited or disregarded.

It is unknown who the two witnesses were. The futurist would contend that the two witnesses are anonymous and are yet to come. There needs to be more evidence to identify the two witnesses with certainty. However, there is no doubt they were empowered. The angel said, "I will give power to my two witnesses, and they will prophesy one thousand two hundred and sixty days, clothed in sackcloth" (11:3). Along with their identity, the content of their prophecy is not revealed. While we do not know the identity of the two prophets, we are confident of the One of whom Moses told the Israelites, "The Lord your God will raise up for you a Prophet like me from your midst" (Deut 18:15). Like much of Revelation, we are left with only enough clues to make it thought-provoking. God reveals the necessary (Acts 1:7, Dan 2, 2 Thess). That Jesus prevails in Revelation is certain.

Imagine the preaching and prophesying of the two witnesses reaching the hearts of some who subsequently repent and upset others who choose to continue violent and irrational behavior. Are these the earth dwellers mentioned in Rev 6:10? It is no wonder why the mighty angel gives them the power to defend themselves. In God's sovereign plan, the beast ascending from the bottomless pit will war with them, overcome them, and kill them. According to Kayle B. De Waal, there are parallels between the

27. Seiss, *Apocalypse*, 250.

witnesses and the beast.[28] Notice that the witnesses were not killed until after they finished their testimony. Their testimony was not cut short. Their bodies will not be allowed to be put into graves, and "those who dwell on the earth will rejoice over them, make merry, and send gifts to one another because these two prophets tormented those who dwell on the earth" (Rev 11:10). The two witnesses stand before the Lord as witnesses for Christ. They stood before the Lord in their testimony, faithful unto death. Ascending to heaven in a cloud, God rewards their fidelity. Matthew writes that Jesus was accused of tormenting two demon-possessed men (Matt 8:29). All Christians must be prepared to confess Christ and risk tormenting unbelievers.

The narrative shifts from what *will* happen to *what* happened without revealing when what happened or will happen. After their dead bodies lay in the streets of spiritually named Sodom and Egypt for everyone to see for three and a half days (half of seven, the number of perfection), God breathed life into them, and the witnesses ascended into Heaven in a cloud. The witnesses' exoneration is resonant with Christ's resurrection-ascension, except the ascension of the witnesses occurred in public view where "great fear fell upon those who saw them" (Rev 11:11). An earthquake followed, one-tenth of the city fell, and seven thousand were killed. [29] In the lament for Israel in Amos 5:3, a tenth was left of the house of Israel, punishment for flagrant, impenitent idolatry. The Lord preserves seven thousand in Israel who have not bowed to Baal (1 Kgs 19:18). Still, seven thousand are killed in the earthquake in Rev 11:13. This partial destruction brings terror to the eyes of the survivors, who then give glory to the God of heaven. Repentance

28. De Waal, "Two Witnesses," 172. The two witnesses prophesy (Rev 11:3), and the beast has two horns and speaks (13:11). The witnesses stand before the Lord (11:4), and the beast of the earth stands before the first beast (13:12); fire proceeds from the mouth of the witness and involves killing (11:5), and the beast makes fire come down, and killing is involved (13:13, 15). The witnesses have power (11:6), and the beast has authority (13:12). The two witnesses are prophets (11:10), and of the beast are false prophets (16:13, 19, 20, 20:10). The witnesses perform signs (11:6), and the beast performs signs (13:13–14, 19:20). The witnesses receive authority from God (11:3), and the beast receives authority from the first beast (13:12). The witnesses torment earth-dwellers (11:10, and the beast deceives earth-dwellers (13:14). God gives breath to the witnesses (11:11), and the beast gives breath to the image of the beast (13:15).

29. Nine-tenths fell in Isa 6:13. Did only a tenth fall in Rev 11:13 because of the work of the witnesses? Can the tenth be considered a tithe? In the lament for Israel in Amos 5:3, a tenth was left of the house of Israel. The Lord reserves seven thousand in Israel who have not bowed to Baal (1 Kgs 19:18), but seven thousand are killed in the earthquake in Rev 11:13.

is not mentioned, but fearing and glorifying God can represent the virtual equivalent (16:9; cf. 11:18; 14:7; 15:4;19:5). The second woe is past. The third woe is coming quickly (Rev 11:14) and is revealed after the seventh trumpet judgment.

## *The Seventh Angel Blows His Trumpet (Rev 11:15–11:19)*

The seventh trumpet sounds as we approach the end of the second cycle of judgment. The twenty-four elders, representing the church in Heaven, who have been sitting before God on their thrones since Rev 1 and have appeared seven times in a similar context, fall on their faces and give thanks to God. Revelation is not providing a strict chronology of end-of-day events, but rather a sequence of events. It is looking at similarities again and again from different perspectives without negating the distinct differences. Revelation shows us the kinds of things that have occurred, are presently happening, and continue to occur until Jesus returns.

The last verse in Rev 11 brings us to the pivotal, theological center of Revelation, "Then the temple of God was opened in Heaven, and the ark of His covenant was seen in His temple. And there were lightnings, noises, thundering, an earthquake, and great hail" (Rev 11:19). Experiencing the temple of God on earth is spectacular. To see both the ark of the covenant and the temple of God in Heaven is titanic. Several Church Fathers interpret this "Ark" as Mary, the Blessed Mother. The ark of the covenant was most sacred.[30] The ark symbolizes God's presence amid His people. There are seven temples in Scripture: Solomon's; the rebuilt temple destroyed in 70 CE; the human body (1 Cor 6); the local church (1 Cor 3); the universal church (Eph 2:19–22); the rebuilt temple in the Tribulation; and the Millennial temple. And now, something usually hidden is being seen by John. The not immediately apparent is going to be revealed.

---

30. In Exod 25:10, Moses receives the command to build an ark of acacia wood. Within this ark were to be placed the tables of the law God was about to give to Moses. Upon the top of the ark, probably not as a lid but above the cap, was a golden plate upon which two cherubim, with raised wings and facing each other, covered the ark. God promises to speak to Moses as often as He shall give him commands about the Israelites from the place between the two cherubim. The ark symbolizes God's presence amid His people, which is the common teaching of the Old Testament.

Chapter Twelve

# Cycle Three

## Seven Symbolic Histories (Rev 12–14)

THE THIRD CYCLE OF visions progresses from a woman in heavenly attire to a great fiery dragon, a male child, the false prophet, the beast of the sea and the beast of the earth, the 144,000, and angelic announcers. Also included in the vision are the archangel Michael, reaping the earth's harvest, and reaping the grapes of wrath. Unlike the cycles of seven seals (5:1–8:1), and seven trumpets (8:2–11:19) these visions have no explicit numbering. The first and second cycles focused on the judgments from God's throne; this cycle illustrates the severe nature of the spiritual conflict.

**Principal Personages: The People of God vs. Satan (Rev 12:1–12:6).**

This section bridges the narrative until the seven bowls are poured out in 15:5–16:21. John stops the rhythm of sevens with a series of visions or signs. Revelation 12 is central to Revelation. It is a cosmic, spiritual battle in Heaven comprising a woman, a child, and a dragon. The woman, a great sign, is pregnant, clothed with the sun, has the moon under her feet, and is wearing a garland of twelve stars on her head. Interestingly, this is like one of Joseph's dreams, "And this time, the sun, the moon, and the eleven stars bowed down to me" (Gen 37:9). The woman is a sign, not a vision, not a wonder. No mere creature, or any number of creatures, can be literally clothed with the sun. The woman's adornment is a pictorial representation, which is to be figuratively understood.

Some believe the woman is the Blessed Virgin Mary or the church. However, in Revelation 12:2, she "cried out in labor and in pain to give birth." In Mariology, labor pain affects only those with original sin, and some claim that Mary did not have original sin; thus, the woman if Mary would be without labor pains. Also, the woman gave birth in Heaven, and Mary gave birth on earth. She cannot represent the church in some respect because the church did not give birth to Christ. However, ordinary Scripture imagery speaks of the church under the figure of a woman, a spouse, or a mother. Therefore, the woman could represent Israel, the bride of Christ, or the church.[1] There are four women mentioned in the book of Revelation: Jezebel, 2:20; this woman in question, 12:1; the harlot, 17:4; and the bride, 19:7. Only this woman in question bore a male Child who was to rule all nations with a rod of iron. The bride in 19:7 is arrayed in fine linen, clean and bright, not with moon and stars and sun. If the bride of Christ is the church, as alluded to in Eph 5:22–33, the mysterious woman might also be the bride in 19:7 after a wardrobe change. The collective body of the church or people of God, in this case, Israel, are indeed assailed by Satan.

Israel is frequently presented as the wife of Yahweh (Jer 3, Ezek 16). Isaiah claims Israel is the source of the Messiah (Is 9:6). In Hos 11, Israel is the child God loved, "And out of Egypt I called My son" (v. 1). Israel is God's firstborn. "Israel *is* My son, My firstborn" (Exod 4:22); that "which was spoken by the Lord through the prophet, saying, 'Out of Egypt I called My Son'" (Matt 2:15). The nation of Israel gave birth to Christ through the Virgin Mary, but if the woman represents Israel, she suffers the dragon's persecution, and the dragon goes to make war with the rest of her offspring, the followers of Christ (Rev 12:17). If the woman does not represent the Virgin Mary, she could represent Eve or Israel.

Whoever the woman is, what she represents is most important. By representing the target of persecution of her seed (Israel and the Messiah) of the past, present, and future, we learn of God's ultimate victory through those who resist the influence of evil. The woman has become a symbol of God's faithful people. Unlike the woman in Rev 17, who lures men to herself, away from God and Christ, this woman seeks to draw men to their Creator and Redeemer.

Perhaps Israel and her offspring are the children of God baptized in the New Testament covenant. Though they shall face the threat of being

---

1. Jere 2:32; 7:34; 16:9; 25:10; and 33:11.

killed, they "keep the commandments of God and hold the testimony of Jesus" (cf. v.11 and 1:9, 6:9; 19:10).[2]

The dragon, Satan, devil, is another sign. The devil (*diabolos* in Greek) is "a great, fiery red dragon having seven heads and ten horns and seven diadems on his heads" (Rev 12:3), all to show "authority." Diadems are ornamental headbands. Using his tail, Satan drew "a third of the stars of heaven and threw them to the earth" (Rev 12:4) and stood before the woman to devour her Child, Jesus. The devil, as a sign, did not sling the stars from the woman's crown or even literal stars. The thrown stars are not a meteor shower. God made and knew the number and names of all the stars, and He multiplies descendants as the stars of Heaven (Gen 1:16; 22:17). The stars fought against the commander of the Canaanite army (Judg 5:20). The male goat representing Greece "cast down some of the host [of heaven] and some of the stars to the ground" (Dan 8:10). A third of the stars were darkened in Rev 8:12. Stars are symbols of angels. Peter refers to the angels God did not spare who sinned and cast them down to hell (2 Pet 2:4). These stars of Heaven could be angelic beings thrown to earth as fallen angels (demons) who intend to consume the baptized (children of God) who are the church in Israel.

Keeping in mind that Christ is eternal, God cast Satan from Heaven centuries before Christ incarnate for wanting to establish a "throne above the stars of God" and "be like the Most High" (Is 14). The desire to be "like God" is the source of all sin (Gen 3:5). We are never more like Satan and less like Jesus than when driven by pride and selfish ambition. If Isa 14 does not describe the fall of Satan, it points to the ultimate defeat of all the forces of evil opposing God and his people. John says the woman and the Devil are both "signs," but John did not write that the Child was a sign. The Child is the reality.[3] The Child, Jesus, is the Messiah,[4] "She bore a male child who was to rule all nations with a rod of iron. And her Child was caught up to God and to the throne of God" (Rev 12:9). In this respect, the woman is symbolic of Mary.

The woman fled into the wilderness to a place God had prepared for her where, perhaps angels, would feed her for 1260 days. The literal length

2. Rogerson, *Commentary*, 1555.

3. Johnson, *Discipleship*, 221.

4. Also prophesied in Mic 5:3, "Therefore He shall give them up, Until the time *that* she who is in labor has given birth; Then the remnant of His brethren Shall return to the children of Israel."

of the Jewish War (66–70 CE) was forty-two months. The people of God flee persecution by scattering across the land. For instance, Israel flees Pharaoh by an exodus into the desert; the Holy family flees from Harrod to Egypt, and the Christians flee Jerusalem from the Romans. The children of God continue to escape the world's evils, the flesh, and demonic powers.

Despite it being written in Rev 12:9 that the dragon is "the serpent of old, called the Devil and Satan, some suppose the enemy dragon represents the Roman Empire, a human, or a nation. In that case, the real enemy remains the dark, spiritual powers at work (the Devil) destroyed by Jesus's followers who remain loving of everyone just as the slain Lamb. The dragon is not a literal dragon, just as the church is not a woman. These dark, spiritual powers are the fallen angels or demons who shall roam the earth seeking the ruin of souls, a prolonged antagonism. Demons belong to the empire of the dragon, the Devil. Evil powers find their place in the realm of Almighty God's creation. God never made an evil being, but He did make moral agents able to do wrong and right. If it is possible for a man to do evil, it is indeed possible for other creatures to do evil. "And they overcame him by the blood of the Lamb and by the word of their testimony" (Rev 12:11).

## History of the Dragon (Rev 12:7–12:12)

War breaks out in heaven between the archangel Michael and the dragon, "that serpent of old, called the Devil and Satan" (Rev 12:9). Michael and his angels fight and overcome the dragon and the dragon's angels. The dragon and his angels can no longer remain in heaven and are cast to the earth. Imagine a war in Heaven and God allowing Satan in His presence, as recorded in Job 1:6. Perhaps it is easier to comprehend if Satan is not present with God in the third heaven. After fourteen years of not mentioning it, Paul professes to have been caught up to the third heaven (2 Cor 12:2). Since a third Heaven exists, there is likely a first and second Heaven, perhaps even more than three. We are not told how many heavens the High Priest passed through (Heb 4:14). Conventional thought is for a first Heaven (the sky), a second Heaven (outer space with the sun, moon, and stars), and the third Heaven (the highest if we are limiting the number of heavens to three) where God sits on His throne. The point is, "We have such a High Priest, who is seated at the right hand of the throne of the Majesty in the heavens" (Heb 8:1). The Devil may deceive men, but he cannot inflict his deceptions and finesses on heaven. "Indeed, Heaven and the highest heavens belong to the Lord your God, also the earth with all that is in it" (Deut 10:14).

## History of the Woman (12:13–17).

The child was caught up to heaven, Satan was relocated from the heavenly realm to the earthly realm, and the woman fled into the wilderness. "A time and times and half a time" is three-and-a-half years or one-thousand two-hundred and sixty days—the duration of time the woman, representing Israel, will be supernaturally nourished and protected from the dragon. She was given two wings of a great eagle and fled to the wilderness. Similarly, God brought Israel to the wilderness on eagles' wings, as it were, and there he fed, cared for, and protected the Israelites (see Exod 16; 17:8–16; 19:4). Did this woman flee to the wilderness in the Sinai peninsula—the same location Habakkuk's prayer portrayed a theophany (Hab 3:3)—the same wilderness Moses fled for security from the wrath of Pharaoh (Exod 2:15)—and to which Elijah went for refuge from the bloody Jezebel (1 Kgs 19)? Perhaps the woman fleeing represents those in Judea commanded to flee to the mountains in Matt 24:15–16. If this woman is to faithfully overcome as did the likes of Antipas, God will nourish her with hidden manna (Rev 2:17).

After being cast to earth and failing to destroy the child, the dragon turned his anger towards Israel and her offspring, the people of Christ. "[T]he serpent spewed water out of his mouth like a flood after the woman" (Rev 12:15). Water spewed is best interpreted symbolically. The Water represents an aggressive assault by Satan, the deceiver, and the accuser (Rev 12:9–10). Satan has spewed forth a flood of deception and lies to destroy the children of God in this world. Satan is relentless. Again and again, he attacks God's children through war, pestilence, and propaganda of lies. References to floodwaters and waters moving like rivers in Jer 46–47 symbolize advancing armies. In this respect, soldiers dispatch to assail, overwhelm, and destroy the woman in retreat. Before the woman fled, the earth opened and swallowed the Water spewed from the dragon just as the Water swallowed the pursuing Egyptians in Exod 15:11–12 and Korah's men and possessions in Num 16:32.

Krodel writes, "The flood of water, spit out by the dragon, is the counter-image to 'the river of the water of life' that flows from the throne of God and from the Lamb through the city of God."[5] Alternatively, in Revelation, the mouth usually refers to speech (1:16; 13:5), and some might interpret this as Satan's attempt to destroy the church by prompting earthly foes of God to utter false words of slander against it or to inspire false brothers to speak words of false teaching within the church. The resultant hatred and persecution are thwarted by God's people remaining faithful and loving. Again, suppose the enemy dragon represents Rome, a human, or a nation. The real enemy is the demonic powers at work that will be conquered by Jesus's followers who remain loving of everyone just as the slain Lamb. "And they overcame him by the blood of the Lamb and by the word of their testimony" (Rev 12:11).

## History of the Beast from the Sea (Rev 13:1–10).

John reveals more about the persecutions in the early symbolism of Daniel's animal visions.[6] The beast of the sea is the first of two beasts and the eighth persecuting king to present themselves in this part of Revelation, where one beast represents the national military power and the other beast the exalting power of the Roman Empire.[7] Scripture frequently associates the sea with evil or the Gentile people (Ps 74:13–14; Matt 8:28–31). The beast of the sea is the same beast that rose out of the Abyss in Rev 11:7 to persecute the two witnesses. In this regard, one can interpret the two witnesses not as persons but as two lampstands among the seven golden lampstands in 2:1. If the seven golden lampstands symbolize the seven churches in Asia Minor, then perhaps the two lampstands might symbolize the church of Smyrna and the church of Philadelphia, neither of which were rebuked by Jesus. "He who is upright in the way is an abomination to the wicked" (Prov 29:27).

As early as 27 BCE, most Roman emperors insisted on being worshipped above other gods.[8] The dragon empowers the beasts, and the three form a sort of "unholy trinity." The beast of the earth is a false, blasphemous prophet, the beast of the sea is an antichrist, and the dragon is Satan—an unholy trinity. The beast from the sea has seven heads, ten horns, and ten crowns on his horns. This beast is like a leopard with the feet of a bear and

5. Krodel, *Revelation*, 245.

6. Based on Dan 7:1–8.

7. I explain more about the eighth king in later chapters.

8. Johnson, *Discipleship*, 234.

the mouth of a lion.[9] One might see a connection between the beast being healed (Rev 13:3) and Jesus the Lamb resurrected, especially if the beast coming out of the abyss is viewed as rising from the dead. If the beast of the sea is considered the Roman Empire or Rome, as alluded to in Dan 7, a revived Roman Empire could be considered resurrected. The fourth beast in Dan 7 is like the first in Revelation, the beast of the sea. Daniel explains to Nebuchadnezzar, "after you shall arise another kingdom inferior to yours; then another, a third kingdom of bronze, which shall rule over all the earth" (Dan 2:39).

Daniel had a dream of four beasts coming out of the sea. One was like a lion, the other like a bear, the third like a leopard, and the fourth differed from all the beasts before it. The four beasts might correspond closely to the four kingdoms of Nebuchadnezzar's dream. The first kingdom, gold, could be Babylon 606 BCE – 539 BCE. The second kingdom, silver, could be Persia 539 BCE – 332 BCE. The third kingdom, brass, could be Greece 332 BCE – 68 BCE. The fourth kingdom, "strong as iron . . . that kingdom will break in pieces and crush all the others" (Dan 7:40), might be Rome. The main point here is that another kingdom, one set up by God, "shall never be destroyed . . . and [this kingdom] will consume all these kingdoms, and it shall stand forever" (Dan 2:44). Therefore, this fourth beast of Nebuchadnezzar's dream in Dan 2 and Daniel's vision in Dan 7 is the last beast before the Son of Man comes with the clouds of Heaven who will be joined by the Saints of the Most High to triumph in the fall of the beasts under the judgment of God (Zech 14:1–4; Rev 13:7–17; 19:20).

In Rev 13, John conveys to his readers that the beast symbolizes a world kingdom. This beast rules for forty-two months, the same time the witnesses prophesied before being left dead in the street for three days and the amount of time the woman was nourished in the wilderness. The beast

---

9. In Dan 7:1–11, Daniel sees the lion, bear, and leopard as three separate beasts, along with the fourth beast having the ten horns, "a fourth beast, dreadful and terrible, exceedingly strong. It had huge iron teeth; it was devouring, breaking in pieces, and trampling the residue with its feet. It *was* different from all the beasts that *were* before it, and it had ten horns. I was considering the horns, and there was another horn, a little one, coming up among them, before whom three of the first horns were plucked out by the roots. And there, in this horn, *were* eyes like the eyes of a man, and a mouth speaking pompous words" (Dan 7:7–8). This beast is defeated, but the other three remain for a time. "I watched till the beast was slain, and its body destroyed and given to the burning flame. As for the rest of the beasts, they had their dominion taken away, yet their lives were prolonged for a season and a time" (Dan 7:11–12). Revelation 13 can be more fully understood after examining Daniel's prophecy.

of the sea blasphemies against God, His name, His tabernacle, and those who dwell in Heaven (13:6). Rising out of the chaos of the sea, this beast is symbolic of rebellion. The beast of the sea has political power manipulated by the dragon. Some say it represents military power, and some say it symbolizes Rome. The latter is most probable since the Roman Empire had long been dead in history (as John looks backward). [10]

If this beast with the mortally-wounded-but-healed head is the antichrist, a preterist might think it is emperor Nero. After Nero committed suicide, a contemporary myth among John's audience was that Nero would return from the dead. The prophecies of Daniel and Paul's letters to the early church are references to the beast. In Daniel's vision, the beast has a little horn coming up from among the ten, with eyes like the "eyes of a man and a mouth speaking pompous words" (Dan 7:5–8). The beast ministered to ten thousand times ten thousand but was destroyed, and the dominions of the rest of the beasts were taken away (Dan 7:10–12). Before that, however, this antichrist imitates or counterfeits Jesus Christ so well that he continues his authority for forty-two months or three-and-one-half years.[11] The beast of the sea in Rev 13:5–10 speaking blasphemies against God connects him with the "horn which had eyes and a mouth which spoke pompous words, whose appearance was greater than his fellows" (Dan 7:20).

Christians are to obey those in authority. The government is given the power of the sword, but the church is not.[12] Users of the sword are always accountable to God. Paul, the apostle of the Gentiles, instructed his readers to "Let every soul be subject to the governing authorities. For there is no authority except God, and the authorities that exist are appointed by God" (Rom 13:1). John's audience was familiar with Paul's instructions in his letter to the Romans as Peter's to submit to the Roman emperor (1 Pet 2:13). However, Paul's rulers were quite different from the ruthless rulers dominating John's day. There is no contradiction here. Submission to authority is required if it does not involve a violation of the law of God. Paul wrote around 55 CE during the administration of emperor Claudius who played down emperor worship. John wrote years later, during the

10. The first Babylonian attack on Jerusalem was in 597 BCE. The temple fell in 586 BCE, followed by Babylon's fall in 539 BCE. Ezekiel's grim warnings about such had come true.

11. See Dan 7:17–18.

12. Authority over military affairs is sometimes termed "the power of the sword." In the United States, it resides (with some limitations) in the executive branch of the government, headed by the President.

administration of Domitian, who demanded he is acknowledged as Dominus et Deus, "Lord and God."[13]

People under duress might worship a corrupt government, and a government that provides for all the people's needs, is essentially substituting themselves for God. Choosing to serve the beast might have led to short-term success yet brought eternal destruction. We must obey the rulers unless those rulers command us to do what God forbids. The Roman empire had no power except what was given to it by God. The beast from the sea was given authority to act, to wage war, and when the Christian community opposed this, they could expect grief but only for three-and-a-half years. "Here is the patience and the faith of the saints" (Rev 13:10b).

The order in which Daniel describes the beasts is by successive world empires as we advance in time; lion: Babylon, 606 BCE to 539 BCE; bear: Medo-Persia, 539 BCE to 332 BCE; and leopard: Alexandrian Empire of Greece, 332 BCE to 68 BCE.[14] Nations become beasts when they exalt their power and economic security as a false god and then demand total allegiance. The beast in Daniel's day was Babylon which Persia and Greece followed. The beast in John's day was likely Rome. In reverse order, John describes the beasts looking back in time: leopard, bear, then a lion. As we shall see in Rev 17 regarding a revived Roman Empire, John may be seeing the beast in both its historical and prophetic characters. Some believe the beast is the king in Dan 11:36–45.[15] The beast from the sea has no inherent authority. And although the beast gets permission to wage war from the dragon (Rev 13:2; 7), it is under the superintendence of God Almighty.

In a journal article, Harris mentions five views on the identity of the wounded beast. In the Nero Redivivus View, "John and the early church expected an evil Roman Caesar to return to life, with most people identifying this person as Nero."[16] It is unlikely John was taken in by contemporary myth. God's inspired word is true, and the Nero Redivivus View is a theory of the few. The Nonpersonal View holds that the collective, impersonal evil forces increase persecution. This view does not explain why Christians would worship the beast or question, "who is able to make war

13. Johnson, *Discipleship*, 234.

14. The first kingdom (the lion) is Babylon (Dan 2:36–38); The second kingdom (the bear) is Persia (Dan 2:39; 8:20; and 10:13); The third kingdom (the leopard) is Greece (Dan 2:39; 8:21; and 10:20).

15. king and kingdom seem to be used interchangeably.

16. Harris, "Wound of the Beast," 459.

with him?" (13:4). Differing from the Nero Redivivus View, Nero, Judas Iscariot, or some unidentified person returns as a different embodiment in the Reincarnation View. However, Satan can give the domain to whomever he wishes and would not need re-embodiment (Luke 4:6). The remaining views are the Antichrist View and the Revived Roman Empire View.

## History of the Beast from the Earth—the False Prophet (Rev 13:11–18).

Antichrists are already in the world. "For many deceivers have gone out into the world who do not confess Jesus Christ as coming in the flesh. This is a deceiver and an antichrist" (2 John 1:7). The beast from the earth is an antichrist, another of Satan's counterfeit of holy things. Recall that many antichrists will attempt to destroy God's people (1 John 2:18, 22; 4:3; and 2 John 7). Scriptural references establishing that there is more than one Antichrist, that he denies the incarnation of Christ, and that the Antichrist is the evil one includes 2 Thess 2:3–8; Rev 13 and 19:20; Matt 24; and Dan 8 and 9:27.

The beast from the earth is part of the unholy trinity and exercises all the authority of the beast of the sea but causes the earth and those who dwell in it to worship the beast of the sea, the false messiah or anti-Christ. The beast from the earth had two horns like a lamb and spoke like a dragon. The dragon mimics God the Father as the anti-God.[17] This beast from the earth having two horns (horns are the image of strength), dragon voice, full authority, ability to perform great signs, is the anti-Holy Spirit, the beast that mimics the Holy Spirit, "so that he even makes fire come down from Heaven on the earth in the sight of men" (13:13). [18] Extrabiblical literature notwithstanding, it is evident from Job 40:15–41:34 that the beast from the sea and the beast from the earth are commonplace in ancient Jewish literature.

The dragon and the two beasts are Hell's Trinity in Unity. Many commentators attempt to identify Hell's Trinity as including the Roman clergy, the papal kingdom, or the French Republic. The unholy trinity attempts to destroy the believers of the Holy Trinity, a Trinity of one Father, one Son, and one Holy Spirit: One God in three coeternal Persons. The unholy trinity is united as false prophets and antichrists. Jesus told his disciples, "For

17. Seiss, *Apocalypse*, 332.

18. Johnson, *Discipleship*, 242.

false Christs and false prophets will rise and show great signs and wonders to deceive, if possible, even the elect" (Matt 24:24). The unholy trinity could be a person. The beast of the earth is declared as a false prophet in Rev 16:13, 19:20, and 20:10. However, the beast as a composite of false prophets and not an individual is symbolic of a corporate system with an individual administrator. Some commentaries suggest this corporate system is the Roman Catholic Church, a Historicist view of this part of Revelation. Gregg states, "After the establishment of Roman Catholic domination in the sixth century, the Bishop of Rome would do anything in his power to maintain and expand his influence."[19] To bring the whole world under the influence of Rome, the Roman Catholic Church (as the beast of the sea) would have to be revered and seen as holy. The beast would have to be like Jesus, the Lamb, as in Rev 13:11, where the beast has "two horns like a Lamb."

Gregg suggests a connection between features of the Roman Catholic Pope's vestment and the antichrist. Lamb's wool is used in the vestment, and the inference is to the Pope as the lamb as Jesus is the Lamb. Thus, the beast would have to be like Jesus, the Lamb. As quoted by Miller, Schoenig offers a narrative of the evolution of the woolen liturgical band called the pallium. The Pope, archbishops, and some bishops in the Roman Catholic Church wear the pallium around their necks and over the chasuble to symbolize their participation in papal authority. Initially, donning the pallium was without any real significance but gradually moved to more decisive importance. From crux to requirement to honorary to badge, the pallium changed radically from the sixth to the twelfth century as a systematized feature of religious authority.[20]

The idea of papal authority linked to the antichrist stemmed from works incorporating nominal tropes, anatomical metaphors, and antithetical concepts. After university professor and preacher Jan Huss (1369–1415 CE) launched his treatise known as *Anatomy of the Antichrist,* he attended the Council of Constance (1414–18) for a hearing and was subsequently seized and burned at the stake for heresy against the doctrines of the Roman Catholic Church. German theologian Philip Melanchthon was diplomatically critical of Catholics. The content of his disputatious writings and speeches closely paralleled that of *Anatomy of the Antichrist.* "Although Melanchthon rejected scholastic theology, he did appreciate the theology of Augustin that emphasized the radical nature of sin and the importance

19. Gregg, *Revelation,* 350.
20. Miller, "Bonds of Wool," 198.

of grace."[21] The Middle Ages lasted approximately from the 5th to the late 15th centuries. "By the end of the Middle Ages, the idea of the papal Antichrist had developed as a complex concept with multiple layers of meaning and with its vocabulary and rhetorical tropes."[22] The answer to what linked Roman Catholicism to the antichrist lies in understanding the past.

The many church fathers of the Middle Ages continuously probed and refined church doctrine. Leading up to the Protestant Reformation of 1517, and continuing past the 19th century, the ideas of theologians, such as Augustine, were seriously challenged by other theologians attempting to differentiate between the teachings of Jesus and those of church tradition. For example, Jesus taught through Paul that "by grace you have been saved through faith, and that not of yourselves; it is the gift of God" (Eph 2:8). Augustine and Thomas Aquinas agreed that justification is by God's grace and is not merit-based. However, the Catholic church began to sell indulgences, and by giving money to the church, one could buy salvation. Luther and other reformers rejected this corruption and focused their theology on justification by faith and faith alone. God is the first cause, and humans are not. Luther, Augustine, and Aquinas agreed that God's grace freely gives faith, and without God's grace there can be no justification. All three agree that faith is the work of God and not the work of the person. Justification moves one from a state of sin to a state of grace and salvation—something indulgences cannot provide.

The doctrine of justification is one example of where there was a bit of unity between Protestants and Catholics. If not for the mistranslation of "works," there could be accord in faith without works is dead of James 2:14–26. The discord in theology became apparent in what is believed to occur after justification. Luther's understanding is that justification is relational; justification does not change the nature of one fallen by original sin. Aquinas and Augustine reason that justification changes one's nature; as one moves away from sin, one's nature becomes more righteous to God. Nowhere in Scripture does grace heal human nature. Moses experienced God's grace for 120 years, yet disobeyed, failed to trust God, and never entered the promised land (Deut 34:7; Num 20:2–13; 27:12–14; and Deut 32:51). There was none greater than John the Baptist, but even the least in the kingdom of heaven is greater. John the Baptist was filled with the Holy Ghost but doubted Jesus (Luke 7:20–23). Moses, John the Baptist, and

21. Wyk, "Philip Melanchthon: A Short Introduction," 4.

22. Buck, "Anatomia Antichristi," 349.

many more grace-filled righteous humans, naturally succumbed to sin and eventually died. There is no indication that justification changed their nature. There is, however, every indication that they were justified righteous while battling the sinful nature of fallen man.

When the Reformers confronted the doctrine of justification along with the number of sacraments, books of the Bible, the doctrine of original sin, the authority of church tradition, and the eucharist, the church convened the Council of Trent to address these and other issues, including the authority of the Pope. Again, the Reformers focused their theology on the teachings of Jesus and not on church tradition. "Christ always stood for poverty, humility, and perfection while the Pope evinced wealth, simony, and lust for power."[23] Before and in addition to the Protestant Reformers were the Catholic Reformers who desired to stop financial abuses, educate cleric, and focus on the moral and spiritual health within the church. The Protestant Reformers were concerned with doctrinal and structural reforms, and "believed the problems in the Church were not merely due to moral laxity."[24] The Council of Trent, prompted by the Protestant Reformation, was the most important movement in clarifying issues within the Catholic church but did little to resolve the issues presented by the Protestant Reformers.

Radical reactions and misunderstandings between Catholics and Protestants during the 15th century led to the current schism. The Council of Trent seemed to concede that there were abuses concerning the beliefs and practices, such as holy orders, confirmation, the Eucharist, penance, and extreme unction (anointing the sick). Fastiggi writes, "The response of the council, though, was to respond to the abuses rather than to reject Catholic beliefs."[25] The Council of Trent established many rules and teaching to root out any abuse or the perception thereof which included declaring many of the Protestant interpretations as anathematic. This reaction led to cementing the schism. According to Lawrence, "the Council of Trent nailed the lid on the coffin of religious unity, and the Roman Church emerged as a denomination where examination and questioning of theology was no longer permitted."[26] In number 882 of the Catechism of the Catholic Church (CCC), the Pope is the "pastor of the entire Church [and] has full, supreme,

23. Buck, "Anatomia Antichristi," 350–51.

24. Fastiggi, "Contributions of the Council of Trent," 4.

25. Fastiggi, "Contributions of the Council of Trent," 9.

26. Lawrence, "Medieval Refinements in Augustinian Theology," 61.

and universal power over the whole Church." Here is where the perception may lie between the Pope and the antichrist.

Daniel, the Jewish prophet of the Old Testament, alluded to the persecution of the Jews during the full and universal power of Antiochus IV Epiphanes. The term "antichrist" is not used in the Bible until 1 John 2:22, but some claim the antichrist is depicted in Dan 7. Any person, nation, or system substituting themselves in Christ's place is considered an antichrist. It is the antithesis of the true Christ if one embodies wickedness, works fraudulent wonders, or even authenticates fraudulent works, as Christ worked true ones. This includes the Pope, the exceedingly powerful fourth beast in Dan 7:7, the little horn in Dan 7:8, the "man of sin" in 2 Thess 2:3, or the Roman Empire. In the Bull, "by providence of God, Pope," the twenty-fifth session of the Council of Trent prohibited all men, under pain of excommunication or interdiction, to publish any form of interpretation or commentary on the canon or decrees without approval.[27]

Arand contemplates the papacy and writes, "Controversies will continue to arise because Rome refuses to examine and adjudge fairly the questions raised by the Reformation. Churches cannot be maintained only by force of arms."[28] It is not written in the Catechism of the Catholic Church but according to Robinson, "sixteenth-century popes assumed the title, 'Our lord God the Pope.'"[29] Although it has since been removed from the Westminster Confession, Hutchens claims it was once written in chapter 25 of that Confession that the Pope is the Antichrist.[30] It is obvious, even to the casual observer of Catholicism, that the Pope yields significant power. Luther notes that if the Pope exercised absolute authority, more divisions and sects would inevitably result. Ironically, there are now nearly 34,000 Protestant denominations and sects.[31] Again, the antichrist is antithetical of the true Christ. The evidence for the existence of *the* Antichrist to date is insufficient. However, evidence of Christophobia or Christianophobia abounds.

It is in Rev 13 that we explore the number 666 and learn about the mark of the beast. The mark of the beast in Rev 13:16 is probably not a literal mark on anyone's forehead, right hand, or a physical mark anywhere

27. Council of Trent, "Session 25," 288–89.

28. Arand, "Antichrist?," 394.

29. Robinson, "Identifying the Beast," 593.

30. Hutchens, "Important Denouncement," 5.

31. Arand, "Antichrist?," 397.

else any more than is "His Father's name written on their foreheads" found in Rev 14:1. Speculations of such miss the main point of spiritual distinction. The likes of killer, pedophile, or thief carries a "mark" just as much embedded under the skin as is the mark of the saving grace of Jesus Christ and redemption for a disciple. It is the character of such, not the physical nature of markings or dress. The moral identification and insight are of more practical worth than is the numerical spelling of the beast's name. It is not easy to put a name to the 666. "Here is wisdom. Let him who has understanding calculate the number of the beast, for it is the number of a man: His number is 666" (Rev 13:18). It is fuel for amusement as well as an interesting "game" or "puzzle" for many to tinker with in trying to assign a name.

The first game or puzzle, and the only one to consider, is called gematria, using numbers to spell words. While gematria was used periodically in the Talmud and Midrash, it was not central to rabbinic literature. It is, however, essential to Kabbalah, the Jewish mystical tradition. The rabbis occasionally employed gematria to help support biblical exegesis but did not rely on it heavily. Ronald Eisenberg writes, "The Rabbis of the second century, following the Greek system, gave each of the 22 letters of the Hebrew alphabet a numerical value. The letters *aleph* to *tet* represent the digits 1 to 9; *yud* to *tzadi* from 10 to 90; *kupf* to *tav* from 100 to 400."[32] Much has been said about the "mark of the beast" and its secret number. Consider the contrast between the allegiance mark of the beast and the Shema, the Jewish prayer of allegiance given in Deut 6:4–8 in which "You shall bind them as a sign on your hand, and they shall be as frontlets between your eyes" (Deut 6:8). Jews since before the time of Christ have taken these verses literally and tie small boxes, *Tefillin*, containing these verses on their arms and foreheads. Perhaps the 666 can be viewed as "anti-Shema." The Hebrew alphabet in numerology is presented here with the numerical calculation of the emperor Nero. Numerical values are only assigned to the consonants.

The Hebrew Alphabet in Numerology

1 Aleph א

2 Bet ב

3 Gimel ג

4 Daleth ד

5 Heh ה

6 Vav ו

---

32. Eisenberg, *What the Rabbis Said,* 306.

7 hyin ז

8 Het ח

9 Tet ט

10 Yud י

20 Kaf כ

30 Lamed ל

40 Mem מ

50 Nun נ

60 Samech ס

70 Ayin ע

8 Peh פ

90 Tzady צ

100 Koof ק

200 Reish ר

If you translate the name of one of the most "bestial" of the emperors, Nero Caesar, in the Hebrew alphabet as *nron qsr,* it calculates to 666: N (50), R (200), W (6),[33] N (50), Q (100), S (60), R (200) = 666. Author Darrell W. Johnson writes, "Is the 666 referring to Nero? Likely not. It requires too much playing around with the facts. It requires John's first readers to go from Latin to Greek to Hebrew, and to fudge some letters along the way."[34] Transliteration from Aramaic would add complication.

## A Song of Victory—The 144,000 (Rev 14:1–5).

Revelation 14 reveals a Lamb standing on Mount Zion with 144,000 saints. The voice from Heaven might imply an earthly scene such as at least twenty other verses implying "I heard a voice from heaven."[35] However, the 144,000, likely male, are those redeemed from the earth and not defiled by women, "for they are virgins" (Rev 14:4b). They were without fault before the throne of God. God's throne is in heaven and *is* heaven (Is 66:1; Ps 11:4; Matt 5:34). If they are married men, they are not virgins, but they are also not defiled by their wives. In this respect, "virgins" must represent spiritual purity. They are followers of Jesus. They are the Lamb's followers.[36]

33. The sixth letter of the Hebrew alphabet is Vov/Waw and has the sound of "oh" or "oo."

34. Johnson, *Discipleship,* 248.

35. 2 Sam 22:14; Dan 4:31; Matt 3:17; Luke 3:22; John 12:28, to name a few.

36. The Lamb eventually will transform into the rider on the white horse who slays with the sword of his mouth (Rev 19:11-17) and who rules with a "rod of iron" (Rev 12:5;

Some commentators believe the 144,000 in this chapter are separate from the 144,000 in Rev 7 for two main reasons. First, the members in Rev 7 are sealed and represent all believers, especially those who are martyred for their faith. The Rev 14:1 group had "his name and father's name written on their foreheads." Second, the sealed group is on earth and "do not harm the earth" (7:3). The Rev 14 group is in Heaven, "before the throne of God" (14:5), where John hears the harps playing and singing before the throne, with the four living creatures, the elders, and "the hundred and forty-four thousand who were redeemed from the earth" (Rev 14:1–3).[37]

If the 144,000 is figurative or symbolic, could they represent the godly nucleus beyond just Israel? Revelation 7:4 tells us the 144,000 are "all of the tribes of the children of Israel," twelve thousand from each of the twelve tribes of Israel. Therefore, they would not be separate groups, and they are all Jews. They are token of the redemption of the saintly nations and the glory that is to unfold in the kingdom. We are to be holy and blameless before God (Eph 1:4). If 144,000 represents a larger-than-large number, then one would be wise to emulate those among the 144,000.

The significance of "not defiled by women" is not altogether clear. Celibacy is not required to be among the sealed or redeemed. Perhaps the soldiers in holy wars were expected to abstain (see Deut 20; 23:9–10; 1 Sam 21:5; 2 Sam 11:11), or were celibate priests, or abstinence is a symbolic rejection of the emperor's cult of idol worship in terms of prostitution and adultery. Witherington suggests the 144,000 "virgins" are spiritually pure and loyal.[38] The company of the redeemed were not soiled by the mark of the beast, the worship of idols, or the beasts' dupes into perdition.

There is no biblical evidence to suggest there are two different bodies of people. The details of the group in Rev 7 are effectuated in Rev 14. John uses literary devices in Revelation. According to Huber, John reveals a community in peril because of growing internal conflicts (Rev 2:2; 14–15) and that religious persecution is on the horizon. Huber goes on to say that John "provides his audience with a series of images with which to imagine its identity, including that of a multitude of male virgins."[39]

---

19:15)

37. The "great multitude which no one could number" are before the throne of God (Rev 7:15).

38. Witherington, *Revelation*, 185–86.

39. Huber "Sexually Explicit?," 3.

The beauty of Rev 14 is that we find King Jesus, the slain Lamb, standing victoriously against the beasty nations. Revelation 14 bookends those sealed, "the tribes of the children of Israel" in Rev 7:4. The 144,000 are Jews and after them John sees a "great multitude which no one could number of all nations, tribes, peoples, and tongues . . . clothed in white robes" (Rev 7:9). The ones clothed in white robes are not identified as Jews only and must include Gentile saints.[40] The entire book of Revelation is sandwiched, with an inclusio or bracket, at the beginning and end of the book. Eight verses into the beginning, we read, "I am the Alpha and the Omega, the Beginning and the End" (Rev 1:8), and towards the end, we read, "I am the Alpha and the Omega, the Beginning and the End" (Rev 21:6).

## Three Angelic Messengers (Rev 14:6–11)

John sees three angels in succession.[41] The first angel proclaims the universal gospel. The second angel announces temporal judgment "Fallen! Fallen is Babylon the Great" (Rev 14:8), and the third angel warns of eternal judgment. This fall of Babylon is not likely among the first falls of the Old or First Babylon Kingdoms mentioned earlier. This fall of Babylon is likely looking forward towards the second coming of Christ. The Angel sets the stage for what is to come in Rev 17.

The third angel refers to the first angel as "another" angel, which implies this is an additional angel to perhaps the seven angels standing before God in Rev 8:2. A different angel to the seven also appears in Rev 14:8, the one who announces, "Babylon is fallen, is fallen." Yet another different angel, a mighty angel of warning, appeared in Rev 10:1. It is uncertain how many angels are present. At least in this section, three of them are flying in "mid-heaven" and telling everyone—every nation, tribe, tongue, and people—to worship God. They proclaim that Babylon has fallen and warn them of the consequences of not following God.[42] First-century Jews often referred to Rome as Babylon. Rome was the pagan power in Peter's

40. See Eph 2:11–22.

41. Although not canonized, extrabiblical literature, such as the Damascus Document and the Words of the Luminaries, provide historical information. The Damascus Document, the only sectarian Qumran document discovered before the Dead Sea Scrolls, describes the activities of the angels but not as well as what John reveals here and throughout Revelation.

42. Can the angels move about freely because this "mid-heaven" has been vacated by Satan's fall to earth?

Day. Peter's reference to "She who is in Babylon" in 1 Pet 5:13, is probably a reference to the church in Rome. Mark, with Peter when he wrote, is known to have been with Paul in Rome.[43] Revelation's Babylon could be Jerusalem but not without difficulties. The traditional interpretation of Babylon, especially for Rev 17 and 18, is Rome.[44]

The angels are not proclaiming a message of salvation but rather the everlasting gospel, and they are letting everyone know that the hour of God's judgment has come. As a Second Temple text, Revelation speaks of angels revealing messages, aiding the righteous, and attending God in heaven. The message foreshadows Rome's defeat which is not explained until Rev 17–18. The evil and immoral pagan empire oppressing John's audience cannot and will not last.

## *Care for the Saints (Rev 14:12–13)*

Here is a direct appeal to the faithful. The saints who keep God's commandments are informed their patience will pay off, and the wicked will be judged soon. Matthew 10:22 also says, "And you will be hated by all for My name's sake. But he who endures to the end will be saved." The saints who die by persecution will find relief, antithetic to the punishment because they who die in the Lord will be blessed. We live by faith, not by sight, and we live eternally only because of the work of Christ. "Thus, Christian conflict with the world is not ultimately bad; for John, it presents an opportunity for radical obedience which, in turn, prepares for the manifestation of God's justice."[45] There are nine beatitudes in Matthew and four in Luke. Revelation 14:13 is the second of seven beatitudes in Revelation.[46] To endure and remain faithful is emphasized throughout Revelation. The patient faithful will have rest and peace following persecution, unlike those who worship the beast who will "have no rest day or night" (Rev 14:11).

43. See Col 4:10; Phil 24; and Pet 5:13.

44. Biguzzi, "Is the Babylon of Revelation," 385.

45. Rogerson, *Commentary*, 1558.

46. Matt 5:3–12; Luke 6:20–23; and Rev 1:3; 14:13; 16:15; 19:9; 20:6; 22:7, 14.

## The Seventh Symbolic History (One Like the Son of Man) unfolds (Rev 14:14–14:20)

Some claim this is John's vision of God's final judgment, the second coming of Christ, with two symbolic harvests. "The harvest is the end of the age" (Matt 13:39). We see similar images of harvest in Joel 3:13, where the critical background text is that wicked nations are ripe for a harvest of judgment. "Thrust in Your sickle and reap, for the time has come for You to reap, for the harvest of the earth is ripe" (Rev 14:15b). This angel is God's messenger telling Jesus to harvest all of humanity; "the earth was reaped" (14:16). Christ's second coming will be on a great white throne (Rev 20:11), with the command voice of an archangel (1 Thess 4:16), and "with the clouds" (Rev 1:7). Here, One like the Son of Man is "on the cloud," perhaps a description of the second coming with Christ presiding over the harvests.

A thought-provoking issue presents itself with reap and harvest. Some commentators argue that never in the Bible is the image of reaping used for judgment; you reap what you want to keep. Therefore, the two actions of the harvest seem to be about salvation.[47] However, "He who sows iniquity will reap sorrow" (Prov 22:8). Who wants to keep sorrow? "You have reaped iniquity" (Ho.10:13). Who wants to keep iniquity? Other scholars posit that the grain and grape harvest represents Jesus's final judgment.[48] One principle of exegesis is to synthesize Scripture with other relevant Scripture. There are plenty of verses where reaping involves reaping (or harvesting) the good (what you want) as well as the bad (what you do not want).[49] Finally, some commentators believe Rev 14:14–16 refers to the harvest of the righteous and Rev 14:17–20 depicts the judgment of the wicked.

Many scholars agree that the reaping in Rev 14 involves two harvests: the harvest of the righteous and the harvest of the wicked.[50] Perhaps the harvest in Rev 14 is the final judgment where the "good" is separated from the "bad." The evangelization of the world, the sheep without a shepherd, is compared to a harvest (Matt 9:36–38; Luke 10:2; cf. Mark 4:29). John may be referring to Joel 3:13 here since it combines a grain and grape harvest,

47. Johnson, *Discipleship*, 263.

48. Rogerson, *Commentary*, 1558.

49. See Lev 19:9; 23:10; Job 4:8; Ps 126:5–6; Prov 22:8; Hos 8:7; 10:12–14; John 4:35–38; 2 Cor 9:6; Gal 6:7–10; Rev 14:14–16.

50. See 22:29; 23:16; 34:21–22; Le 19:9–10; 23:10, 22; Deut 24:19–20; Ruth 1:22; Prov 10:5; 20:4; Isa 9:3–4; 16:9–10; 17:10–11; Jer 5:24; 8:20; 51:33; Hos 6:11; Joel 3:12–13; Matat 9:37–38; 13:30, 39: Mark 4:28–29; John 4:35; Rev 14:15

but it could also be two separate harvests. In ancient Israel, the first fruits of grain were harvested during the overlap of Passover and the Feast of Unleavened bread. Pentecost is the day the LORD baptized the church with the Holy Spirit and fire from heaven. The grain harvest (Rev 14–16) may symbolize the harvest of the righteous, and the grape harvest (Rev 17–20) may symbolize the harvest of the wicked. The grape harvest followed the grain harvest. More importantly, it provides us with a visual of the reaping of the harvest in the second coming of Christ. Ebeling writes, "bread, wine, and oil formed the so-called Mediterranean triad."[51] Unfaithful Israel credits Baal with "grain, new wine, and oil" (Hos 2:8). The order of the harvest is repeated in Deut 8:8, "A land of wheat and barley, of vines and fig trees and pomegranates."

The first harvest is commonly referred to as a grain harvest (Rev 14–16), although not all expositors label it as a "grain" harvest—it may be a harvest of saints. One like the Son of Man having on His head a golden crown is told to "Thrust in Your sickle and reap, for the time has come for You to reap, for the harvest of the earth is ripe" (Rev 14:15). One possibility of this proclamation by the angel and the act of the One who "sat on a cloud" (Jesus?) is the gathering of the saints to salvation. John the Baptizer spoke of a time of threshing when the Lord will "gather the wheat into his barn" (Luke 3:17).[52] Harvests can also be used to describe a gathering to judgment: "The chaff He will burn with unquenchable fire" (Luke 3:17).[53] If the "grain" is the saved saints, perhaps the chaff symbolizes that part of the "old self," the former conduct, leaving the new man which was created according to God (Eph 4:22–24). Notice there is no blood shed in the first harvest.

The second harvest is the grape harvest (Rev 14:17–20). An angel from the altar tells the angel coming out from the temple in heaven to "Thrust in your sharp sickle and gather the clusters of the vine of the earth, for her grapes are fully ripe" (Rev 14:18). The vine of the earth is thrown into the winepress of the "wrath of God." We are not told if the angel coming out of the temple of heaven is "One like the Son of Man," but who else has the power to throw "grapes" into the great winepress of God's wrath? Who but God coming out of the temple in heaven would tell Jesus what to do? In Joel 3:13, the harvest is ripe, the winepress is full, and "their wickedness

51. Ebeling, "Engendering the Israelite Harvests," 187.

52. See Mark 4:26–29 and Matt 13.

53. See Jer 51:33.

is great." Figuratively, the winepress represents God's judgment on His enemies (Is 63:1–3; Joel 3:13; Lam 1:15).

The proclamation by the angel in the grape harvest is the gathering to judgment of those who followed the beast, the antichrist, and the false prophets (Rev 14:9–10). Christ is the true vine (John 15:1); the vine of the earth is symbolic of the reprobate. The winepress was trampled outside the city, and the blood came up to the horses' bridles for 200 miles. It was outside the city where the unclean was taken to an unclean place (Lev 14:33–45). The blood of Jesus was spilled outside the city (Heb 13:12). It is not the sanctified saints who are thrown into the winepress of the wrath of God.

Some commentators suggest that the 144,000 in Rev 14:1, being first fruits to God and the Lamb, were raptured to heaven and, thus, were not among the grain harvest of Rev 14:14–16. If the reasoning is because the 144,000 are with the harpists before the heavenly throne of God, then the harpists, the four living creatures, and the elders in Rev 14:1–3 along with the innumerable multitude in Rev 5:11, would also be absent in the first harvest. The suggestion that the saints, as good seed, were raptured is not biblically supported.

Consider two different Greek uses regarding "ripe." The ripe in the grain harvest used in verse 15, and Luke 8:6, is in the sense of withered, overripe, or dried up, εξηρανθη (exēranthē), possibly representing the long process of salvation, the righteous. The ripe in the grape harvest used in verse 18, and Mark 4:29, is simply ripe, fully ripe, or ripened, ηκμασαν (ēkmasan), possibly representing one ripe for judgment, the wicked.[54]

We find another relevant reaping metaphor in Matt 13:40–43, where Jesus has the angels carefully separate the "wheat" from the weeds or darnels. Some commentators question if the reaper is Jesus in Rev 14 or an angel. The angel who came out from the earthly temple "orders" the One like the Son of Man (the angel from the heavenly temple) to "Thrust in Your sickle and reap" (Rev 14:15).[55] The One like the Son of Man, on a white cloud, and having on His head a golden crown, describes Jesus. Recall, however, that in Rev 4:4, the elders also wore golden crowns. Recall also that in Dan 7:13, "one like the Son of Man" refers only to Jesus, and that Jesus refers to himself over seventy times in the four gospels as "Son of Man."[56] Scripture

---

54. Zuck, *Bible Knowledge*, 965.

55. That angel coming out from the temple likely proceeds from the very presence and righteousness of God.

56. Dan 7:13, where the Ancient of Days refers to God, "I was watching in the night

helps interpret Scripture. Matthew 13:39 says the "reapers are angels." Jesus washed the feet of the disciples; He can certainly assume the position of or empower an angel to reap the wheat from the tares. If the reaper is not Jesus, then the character is a highly significant angel to be on a white cloud and wear a golden crown.

In Matt 3:10, every tree which does not bear good fruit is cut down and thrown into the fire. In Rev 14, the earth's harvest represents the people of the kingdom. The first harvest is a judgment of salvation that characterizes the period, and the second is the final, climactic one of the wicked. The image of judgment as a harvest is expected in the Bible (see Jer 51:33; Hos 6:11; Joel 3:13; Matt 13:30, 39; and Mark 4:29). We get a better image of the judgment in the second harvest with the winepress. The critical message for the first harvest is that Jesus is the Lord of the harvest and judiciously works the separation so that no believer is judged with the unbelievers. We will all stand in judgment. Second Corinthians 5:6–10 describes a judgment for believers, and Rev 20:11–13 describes a judgment of unbelievers. No one is exempt.

The second harvest is a grape harvest, where the sharp sickle is used to "gather the clusters of the vine of the earth, for her grapes are fully ripe" (14:18). Ripe here is ēkmasan, fully grown. In addition to the earlier three angels having the everlasting gospel and the subsequent angel in the first harvest, another angel came out from the altar having power over fire. Could this power over the fire represent an instrument of justice demanded from the cry of the martyrs (those under the altar) in Rev 6:9 after the opening of the fifth seal? Alternatively, perhaps it is in line with 1 Cor 3:13–15, "each one's work will become clear; for the Day will declare it, because it will be revealed by fire; and the fire will test each one's work, of what sort it is." Likely, it could have some relevance to what we shall see in the pouring of the fourth bowl in Rev 16:8, "Then the fourth angel poured out his bowl on the sun, and power was given to him to scorch men with fire." In any case, power over fire indicates the purging judgment of which this angel is capable.

The angel threw the grape clusters and the vine of the earth into the winepress and the winepress was trampled outside the city. "Trampled grapes" is associated with complete destruction.[57] We find this concept

---

visions, And behold, One like the Son of Man, Coming with the clouds of heaven! He came to the Ancient of Days, And they brought him near before Him."

57. Zuck, *Bible Knowledge*, 1213.

in Isa 63:1–6, with the extended metaphor for the day of the Lord: "I have trodden the winepress alone, And from the peoples no one was with Me. For I have trodden them in My anger And trampled them in My fury." The juice pressed out represents war casualties.[58] Joel 3:13 reads, "Put in the sickle, for the harvest is ripe. Come, go down; For the winepress is full, The vats overflow—For their wickedness is great." Jesus is the true vine, the heavenly vine (John 15:1–17), and there can be earthy vine (Rev 14:18) with sour grapes (Jer 31:29).

False gods bring evil deeds and poisonous fruit. Deut 32:32 tells us, "For their vine is of the vine of Sodom And of the fields of Gomorrah; Their grapes are grapes of gall, Their clusters are bitter." Israel and the church are to bear righteous fruit, but we have a vine producing the fruit of evil and corruption in the second harvest. We find more evidence concerning Israel in Ps 80:8, 14–15; Isa 5:2–7; Jer 2:21; Ezek 17:5–8; and Hos 10:1; and concerning the church in John 15:1–6. If the two harvests are simply a preview of what will happen, the final action is fulfilled in Rev 19:15, where the same figure of speech is used where "He Himself treads the winepress of the fierceness and wrath of Almighty God."

Blood reaches as high as the horses' bridles must be seen as anticipation pointed forward to 19:13–15, the return of Christ. This image derives from the Old Testament prophets who used the picture of the blood-red juice sluicing out of the winepress to describe the outpouring of blood in war (Isa. 63:2–6; Joel 3:13; Rev 19:13, 15). Interestingly, the winepress was demonstrated outside the city just as Jesus shed His blood outside the city gate. For the blood to come out for 1600 furlongs, about 200 hundred miles, and up to the horses' bridles, is symbolic of a climactic battle in which an enormous army is expected to come against Christ in a place called *Har Magiddo* (Hebrew for Armageddon). We read about Armageddon in Rev 16 and 19 and realize the battle was never fought! Jesus, through John, is getting the message out that the ultimate judgment of unbelievers is laid low by the omnipotent power of God.

In this vision John sees a grape harvest (14:18). The grapes are cut and thrown into the vat where the wrath of God is trampled out (14:19). In the Old Testament, the remains of a sin offering were to be disposed of outside the camp (Lev 4:12, 21; 9:11; 16:27), and the ook of Hebrews notes

---

58. God's attack was compared to the treading of grapes. Like grapes, Jerusalem's young men were crushed. In His winepress the Lord has trampled the Virgin Daughter of Judah.

that Jesus shed his blood outside the city that he might sanctify the people (Heb 13:11–12). It is only fitting that judgment be pictured outside the city as well. The blood reached the height of a horse's bridle and ran for 1600 stadia or about 200 miles. The symbolic significance of this distance is not clear. Some have suggested that 1600 (4×4×10×10) signifies the complete destruction of the earth's four corners, while others have observed that the length of the Holy Land is 1664 stadia, indicating that the entire nation was judged. The picture is one of unparalleled catastrophe.[59]

Blood has either a cleansing effect (Heb 9:21) or a polluting influence. Blood makes atonement for the soul (Lev 17:11). Blood defiles the land (Lev 35:33). "The sacrificial language is for the Christian tradition a means of re-interpreting the *apparent* defeat of the execution of Jesus and the martyrs at the hands of the Roman authorities (an inferior power) as *in truth* an offering to God (a superior power)."[60] The blood of the martyrs puts them in a unique place with God.

The martyrs were killed because of their righteousness. They are under the altar in Heaven (Rev 6:9), and the revered martyrs are in front of the throne of God (7:14–15). Jesus' sacrificial blood, the blood of the Lamb, the blood of the firstborn from the dead, places him at the right hand of the Father and gives him power unlike any other.

John presents to the seven churches a choice to resist the beast of Babylon and follow the Lamb; otherwise, take the mark, follow the beast, and suffer eternal damnation. [61] The good news is that many do repent, evident in the second woe when they gave glory to the God of Heaven and in Rev 11:15 when "the kingdoms of this world have become the kingdoms of our Lord and His Christ." However, many do not repent and curse God, just as Pharaoh did in the days of Moses. Remember that John stopped the series of sevens with the seventh seal just before Rev 12, where he presented these visions or signs. Out from the seventh seal comes the seven trumpets, and out from the seventh trumpet comes the seven bowls.

59. Elwell, *Evangelical Commentary*, 1219.

60. Decock, "Symbol of Blood," 166–67.

61. The people of God are offered two choices—life or death. See Deut 30:15; Josh 24:15; Matt 7:13.

# Chapter Thirteen

# Cycle Four

## Seven bowls of God's Wrath from the Temple
## (Rev 15 and 16).

AFTER THE FIRST TWO signs in Rev 12—the great sign of the woman and
the sign of a great, fiery dragon—John sees another sign in Heaven, great
and marvelous: seven angels having the seven last plagues. John now moves
from the signs and visions and continues with the seven series and an appropriate replay of seven of the ten plagues of the Exodus.[1] Out of the
temple in Heaven come seven angels, dressed in bright linen with golden
sashes, to pour out the wrath of God on the earth. Resembling the old covenant high priest, these seven angels are central and are not just another
group of seven angels. They have the seven last plagues, and they, "great and
marvelous" have the complete wrath of God. Later, one of these seven angels will say, "Come, I will show you the bride, the Lamb's wife" (Rev 21:9).

In the meantime, John sees something "like a sea of glass mingled
with fire" (15:2). Rev 4:6 records John seeing this same "sea of glass," and
in addition to the four creatures, John now sees the victors, probably the
saints in Heaven standing on this sea of glass which represents the throne
of God. Perhaps the fire represents God's judgments manifested as declared
in the song of Moses and the song of the Lamb in Rev 15:3–4. Note that the

---

1. John may refer to only seven of ten plagues in keeping with the Old Testament
literature of Pss 78:44–51 and 105:28–36, where the recounting of exodus plagues is
shortened from ten to seven.

song is one song and is an allusion to Exod 15, where the Israelites, like the saints, are delivered after plagues sent from God.

The following is a summary of the bowl judgments. God is in the smoke-filled temple, the smoke working as a "curtain" to block the view of His majesty from man.[2] The beast is on his throne on earth, and the angels go forth to earth towards those having the mark of the beast. Notice the similarities between the devastation of the bowls and the trumpets to the regions of creation. The first four trumpets brought devastation of hail and fire, burning green mountains, a star falls, and the sun, moon, and stars are darkened. The first four bowls bring sores to men having the mark, the sea becomes blood, inland waters are contaminated, and power is given to scorch men with fire from the sun. The fifth bowl is poured out "on the throne of the beast and his kingdom became full of darkness; and they gnawed their tongues because of the pain" (Rev 16:10). The sixth bowl is poured out on the river Euphrates, and its water is dried up and brings us to a place called *Armageddon,* where the seventh angel poured out his bowl into the air and brought the cycle of judgments to an end. This event corresponds with Dan 11:44.

Notice the similarities to the plagues in Exodus. Our bibles show ten plagues, but plagues three, six, and nine were not announced to Pharaoh, leaving seven that were. Even after the awful plagues, Pharaoh did not listen to Moses's appeal to free the Israelites so that they could serve the Lord. Here in Revelation, the wicked people of Babylon would not repent of their deeds. They continued to blasphemy the name of God and would not give him glory. Pharaoh at least pleaded for a reprieve after each of the plagues, but the wicked here are utterly oblivious to divine justice behind the work of the plagues. By not repenting, they are participating in the beast's activity and opposing God's divine plan.

Revelation 15 is a prelude to the judgment of the seven bowls. With the bowl judgments summarized to highlight the defiant behavior and the notorious Armageddon, God's judgment is rooted in His perfect righteousness. It is essential to unpack each bowl judgment in Rev 16 and note that the plagues parallel the judgments expressed with the trumpets and the

---

2. God uses the smoke as a curtain to block the view from man of His majesty. He used it in the desert temple tent, He used it at Mt. Sinai, and He used it in the Jerusalem temple. "The temple was filled with smoke from the glory of God and from His power, and no one was able to enter the temple till the seven plagues of the seven angels were completed" (Rev 15:8).

plagues in Exodus. However, the bowl judgments fall on everyone not united to Christ by faith alone (Rev 16:1–16).

The pouring out of the first bowl brings painful sores or ulcers to anyone having the mark of the beast. In the first trumpet judgment, only one-third of the trees and green grass was burned. The similarity here is that judgment is upon a particular group of humans and a particular part of creation. However, the sores recall the sixth plague of boils that God inflicted on the Egyptians (Exod9:9–11).

The second and third bowl, where the waters turn to blood and kill *all* the sea creatures, drives home punishment by blood and involves the second and third trumpet and the first Egyptian plague. The second trumpet tossed *something like* a mountain into the sea, turning only a third to blood and killing only a third of the sea creatures In Exod 7:14–25, Moses turned the water of the Nile into blood, and that first Egyptian plague killed all the fish and poisoned the water. The second and third bowl kill *all* the sea creatures. God's judgement is getting increasingly worse and more devastating as the end times progress. Recall that the water is made bitter by the star Wormwood brought down by the third trumpet in Rev 8:11. Punishment by blood is against those who shed the blood of the saints and prophets (Rev 16:5–6 and Ps. 79:3).

The fourth bowl is poured out on the sun, and men are scorched with fire just as Babylon the harlot will be burned. The angel told John, "And the ten horns which you saw on the beast, these will hate the harlot, make her desolate and naked, eat her flesh and burn her with fire" (Rev 17:16). Babylon the great will fall, "her plagues will come in one day—death and mourning and famine. And she will be utterly burned with fire, for strong is the Lord God who judges her" (Rev 18:8). God promised the repentant would not be scorched: "They shall neither hunger nor thirst, Neither heat nor sun shall strike them; For He who has mercy on them will lead them" (Is 49:10), Moreover, "They shall neither hunger anymore nor thirst anymore; the sun shall not strike them, nor any heat" (Rev 7:16). While the fourth trumpet darkened the sun (as well as the stars and moon) by a third, the fourth bowl intensified the sun.

It is interesting that in Ezekiel's vision of the wicked being slain, the Lord God first fell upon him, and the likeness of fire took him between earth and Heaven and brought him visions of the wicked being slain. In Ezekiel, it is the ones who sigh and cry over all the wicked abominations committed in Jerusalem that receive a mark from the man clothed with linen and having an inkhorn (a priestly figure, probably an angel and scribe) that are to be protected and not slain (Ezek 9:3–7). Those marked out in this way will be protected in the destruction of Jerusalem, just as their forefathers in Egypt were protected by the blood of the Passover lamb (Exod 12:21–23). Again, amidst all the divine judgment, the people of Babylon, these "earth-dwellers," as seen in Rev 9:21, refused to repent.

The fifth bowl, the fifth trumpet, and the ninth plague of Egypt all bring darkness over the earth. The fifth angel poured out his bowl on the throne of the beast, and his kingdom became full of darkness. Yet this "direct attack" did not bring them to their knees. The pain they still suffer is from the sores or ulcers brought on by the first bowl—there is no relief. The outer darkness reflects the inner darkness of those still refusing to repent of their deeds.

In contrast to those having the mark of the saving grace of Jesus Christ, those having the mark of the beast permeate their souls, instilling in them the hostility towards God and His holiness which is characteristic of the beast himself.[3] We become like what we eat, think, and worship. Keep in mind that in the time of these bowl judgments, there is a world government under the control of Satan and the beast. The good news is, then and now, we are getting closer to the second coming of Christ, who declares to those believers on earth who have escaped martyrdom: "Behold, I am coming as a thief. Blessed is he who watches, and keeps his garment, lest he walk naked and they see his shame" (Rev 16:15).[4] Note the first part of this instruction regarding garments as specific to the church of Sardis (Rev 3:4) and the latter regarding nakedness to the church of Laodicea in (Rev 3:18).

The great river Euphrates dries up when the sixth bowl is poured out, likely paving a way for an invasion from the East (China or a Parthian threat?).[5] The Parthians had been in and out of conflict with the Roman Empire since 53 BCE and had defeated the Romans in 63 CE. Removal of the Euphrates barrier clears a path for conquest; something alluded to with the opening of the first seal (Rev 6:2).

3. Beasley-Murray, *Revelation*, 243.

4. Jesus compared His second coming to a thief (Matt 24:43; Luke 12:39) who will overtake those who are not alert or continue to not repent from their deeds, just as He warned the church of Sardis (Rev 3:3).

5. The series of military events described in Dan 11 and specifically 11:40–45, may have something to do with this invasion from the east where "news from the east and the north shall trouble him" (Dan 11:44).

A biblical precedent exists for a river being dried up to let people pass. God did this when He dried up the Red Sea during the exodus of Israel from Egypt.[6] There is a relationship between the sixth bowl and the sixth trumpet and the Euphrates. Revelation 9:13–21 tells us that when the angel sounded the sixth trumpet, an army of two hundred million horsemen is loosed to slay one-third of humanity.

The time between the trumpet judgments and the bowl judgments may be days rather than months or years. With the advent of the sixth bowl, three unclean spirits— perhaps an unholy trinity—spirits of demons like frogs (like the second plague in Exod 7:17–18) come out of the dragon's mouth. The Great City is divided into three parts (Rev 16:19). The three parts are not named or explained. Is there any correlation between these three parts and the three unclean spirits in 16:13? Are the three parts mounds or hills? The unclean spirits go forth to the kings of the earth and the whole world and gather them for a great battle in Armageddon. Megiddo is in the Jezreel Valley which is currently "split into three sections: Mount Tabor to the north, Mount Gilboa to the south, and the Hill of Moreh in between."[7] The sixth bowl unleashes resistance against God, not an invasion of Rome or Jerusalem (Great Babylon), as some would argue. "The kings of the earth set themselves, And the rulers take counsel together, Against the Lord and against His Anointed" (Ps.2:2).

The word *Armageddon* comes from the Hebrew expression meaning "mound" or "mountain" (*har*) of Megiddo. Eric H. Cline writes, "By the Middle Ages, multiple nationalities, languages, and centuries had added an *n* and dropped the *h*, transforming *Har Megiddo* to *Harmageddon* and thence to *Armageddon*."[8] Adding the "n" *Har Meggiddo* becomes *Har Meggiddon*, and dropping the "h" from *Har* becomes *Armageddon*. Roland E. Loasby writes that the translator recognized the word *har*, mountain, "so he transliterated the whole expression, and it appears in the Greek NT with the addition of *ōn*, as Αρμαγεδων. This again has been transliterated from Greek as Armageddon, with the *h* left off and an additional *d* added, no doubt due to the translator's obsession with Megiddo."[9] Loasby agrees that Har-Magedon is the locality of the battle, but claims the wicked will be destroyed at Mount Zion. Mount Zion is also referred to as the City

6. Wiersbe, *Wiersbe's Expository Outlines,* 843.

7. Cline, *Battles of Armageddon,* 10.

8. Cline, *Digging Up Armageddon,* xiv.

9. Loasby, "'Har-Magedon,'" 132.

of David, and Zion became known as all of Jerusalem. "When the site of Megiddo was excavated in the 20th century, 20 levels of occupation were discovered."[10] Canaanites, Egyptians, Philistines, and Israelites possessed the town in turns dating from the 4th century B.C.

According to Joel 3:1–2, God will enter judgment on the captives of Judah and Jerusalem, and all the nations, in the Valley of Jehoshaphat, "the valley of decision" (Joel 3:14). According to Donald Rappe, "The Hebrew Scriptures are not specific about the location of Jehoshaphat, but the subject of Joel's prophecy is clearly the restoration of Judah and Jerusalem (3:1). Over time, however, a rich and diverse array of traditions emanating from Judaism, Christianity, and Islam identifies it as the Kidron Valley on Jerusalem's eastern flank."[11]

Har Megiddo, "hill Megiddo," is a city at the end of the Plain of Esdraelon (the Jezreel Valley), located 90 km (56 miles) north of Jerusalem and 31 km (19 miles) southeast of the city of Haifa. Mount Megiddo should be named "*Mound* Megiddo" since it is not a mountain but rather a mound formed by over twenty layers of ancient settlement ruins.[12] The city is thought to have seen more battles than any other location in the world. "Many critical battles took place at Megiddo, one of the most strategic cities in the region now called Palestine."[13]

The Jezreel Valley, about 20 miles long and 12–15 miles wide, is shaped like an arrowhead, with the tip at the Plain of Acco pointing northwest toward Mount Carmel. Megiddo is midway along the western edge. Bethlehem and Nazareth are at the northern edge, and Beth Shean, where King Saul and his sons hung from the city walls, is east of the valley, near the base of the arrowhead shape. The Harod Valley is the shaft of the arrow running along the north side of Mount Gilboa and crossing the Jordon River, which runs north and south. Charles H. Dyer writes, "The city of Megiddo was very large, and the site guarded a strategic pass through Mount Carmel. The king of Megiddo was one of thirty-one kings defeated by Joshua during Israel's conquest of Canaan."[14]

10. Camille, "Final Battle," 48.

11. Rappe, "Gathering Place," 365.

12. Dunn and Rogerson, *Eerdmans Commentary*, 22.

13. Kaiser and Garrett, *Archaeological Study Bible*, 1541.

14. Dyer and Hatteberg, *Christian Traveler's Guide*, 39.

The seventh angel poured out his bowl into the air [15] which brings the cycle of judgments to an end and shares the description of Christ's second coming revealed with the sounding of the seventh trumpet (Rev 11:15–19) and draws on the language of the seventh Egyptian plague, hail (Exod 9:17–35). Some view Rev 16:17–21 as the last stage of the tribulation. However, this cannot be the final chapter of the outpouring of God's wrath on the world because in Rev 20:7–8, "Satan will be released from his prison and will go out to deceive the nations."

When Jesus used the phrase, "It is finished" in John 19:30, the Greek word *telelestai* is used which implies a fulfilled payment. When John writes, "It is done" in Rev 16:17, the Greek word *gegonen* is used, which means something is completed or finished. In the end, evil is destroyed, ended, done, but new life is begun. Judgment is coming for those who have not accepted Jesus as their savior. After John uses the words "It is done" or "It is finished" there was a great earthquake, greater than any other (Rev 16:18). This earthquake supersedes all the other earthquakes, more than the fifteen mentioned in Scripture. Along with the earthquake, cosmic symbolism takes center stage when cities of the nation's fall, islands drift away, mountains are moved, and boulders of hail fall upon man. God's wrath is poured out on the idolatrous nation, Babylon. Some expositors claim that the "cup of the fury of his wrath" is specifically directed at Rome and use Rev 14:8: "Babylon is fallen, is fallen, that great city" as support.[16] However, the word "Rome" is not used in Revelation, and Babylon by extension, describes a corrupt and immoral world system of which Rome is but one participant. Therefore, the symbolism of Babylon is applicable to many locations. Moreover, scriptural references to the "great city" are Gibeon (Jere. 22:8 and Josh 10:2), Nineveh (Jonah 1:2, 3:2, 3:3, and 4:11) Jerusalem, by extension (Rev 11:8), and even Babylon specifically (Rev 14:8, 16:19, 17:18, 18:10, 16, 18, 21, and 21:10). The point is bowl judgments are God's judgments against evildoers primarily throughout the Roman Empire. Each of the cities of Asia Minor can be a small manifestation of Babylon. A better picture of God's judgment against "Babylon" lies in Rev 17–19:10.

15. Echoing Eph 2:1–2, "And you *He made alive,* who were dead in trespasses and sins, in which you once walked according to the course of this world, according to the prince of the power of the air, the spirit who now works in the sons of disobedience."

16. Rogerson, *Commentary,* 1561.

# Chapter Fourteen

# Cycle Five

## Judgment on Babylon and Vindication of the Church
### (Rev 17:1–19:10)

REVELATION 17 AND 18 bring no new events, and again we are reminded that Revelation is not written in chronological order. In these chapters, John takes us back to the fall of Babylon to recap and elaborate on some Old Testament visions. When reading Rev 17 and 18 we will rightly think it belongs before or along with the destruction of Babylon in the seventh bowl (Rev 16:17–21) because we will read again about the fall of Babylon in Rev 18. "Babylons" will come and go until Jesus returns to replace the kingdom of Babylon with the Kingdom of Jesus. Revelation 17 addresses the religiosity or spirituality of Babylon, and Rev 18 focuses on the commerce or materialism of Babylon.

John's vision begins with one of the seven angels who had one of the bowls. The angel took him in the Spirit, John's third of four "in-the-Spirit" experiences,[1] to witness this evil woman, a woman full of abominations and the filthiness of her fornication, drunk with the blood of saints (Rev 17:6). Unlike the woman we saw in Rev 12 who seeks to draw men to their Creator and Redeemer, this woman draws men to herself, away from God and Christ. She will be destroyed along with spiritual adulterers.

There are four women mentioned in the book of Revelation: Jezebel, 2:20; the woman clothed with the sun who is perhaps Old Testament Israel, 12:1; the harlot, 17:4; and the bride, 19:7. If we suspect John is referencing

1. See John 1:10; 4:2; 17:3; and 21:10.

Isa 1:21, *"How the faithful city has become a harlot! It was full of justice; Righteousness lodged in it, But now murderers"* we might conclude that Jerusalem represents the faithful city. However, just as corrupt and immoral communities might represent Babylon, any community demonstrating righteousness and commitment to God might represent the "faithful city." A good case can certainly be made for the faithful city to be Jerusalem. Still, even later in Isa 1:27, the righteous and faithful city is identified as Zion rather than Jerusalem, a title that emphasizes the spiritual purpose of Jerusalem. The concept of two immoral cities is found in Ezek 16 and 23, where "Oholah" is Samaria, the capital of the northern kingdom, and "Oholibah" is Jerusalem, the capital of the southern kingdom. In this regard, the harlot is first-century Jerusalem, a preterist position. Commentators who hold this view include David Chilton, Massyngberde Ford, Kenneth Gentry, Scott Hahn, Hank Hanegraaff, R. C. Sproul, and N. T. Wright.[2]

The "mother of harlots" on the scarlet beast represents Babylon the Great.[3] Regardless of the reference to Babylon the Great as Rome, the Roman Empire, Constantinople, Jerusalem, or any other city on seven mountains, this beast is going to Perdition (Rev 17:11). [4] The scarlet beast is evidently the same beast as in Rev 13:1–10, the beast of the sea. John draws from many Old Testament passages having locations of immorality such as those found in Isa 13, 23, 34, and 47; Jer 50–51; and Ezek 26–27. Fittingly, the woman representing false religion, sexual immorality, and idolatry is sitting above and in control of the beast as a government. "And the woman whom you saw is that great city which reigns over the kings of the earth" (Rev 17:18). Several Old Testament references to Jerusalem or Israel as a harlot include Isa 1:21; Jer 2:20; 5:7; Ezek 16; 23; Hos 2:5; 3:3; 4:15; and Mic 1:7. However, Isa 23:16–17 refers to Tyre as a harlot, and Nah 3:4 refers to Nineveh as a harlot. Rev 17:15, regarding where the harlot sits, reveals the harlot's influence beyond Jerusalem or Israel: "The waters which you saw, where the harlot sits, are peoples, multitudes, nations, and tongues."

John writes much about the woman's description, but the angel, "the mind which has wisdom," presents the more meaningful explanation of the beast. Some expositors associate the symbology of "the seven heads are seven mountains" in Rev 17:9 with Rome being built on seven mountains

---

2. Woods, "Have the Prophecies," 80.

3. Rev 17:5.

4. Perdition: hell, purgatory, punishment, abyss, inferno, underworld, hades, nether world.

or hills. However, Constantinople, the capital city of the Roman Empire (330–395 CE), was also built on seven hills.[5] Remember, the symbology of Revelation can be viewed past, present, and future. John identifies the book as a "prophesy" several times (Rev 1:3; 19:10; 22:7, 10, 18, 19).

In addition to the seven mountains, the angel says, "There are also seven kings" (Rev 17:10). Recall from my introduction that I have taken the later-date position where John scribed Revelation after the destruction of Jerusalem and the temple in 70 CE. This position rules out the seven kings being the first five emperors, beginning with Julius Caesar (not actually an emperor), the sixth being Nero, and the seventh coming soon at the very end. Reference to "is himself also the eighth" in Rev 17:11 would then be based on the myth of a "revisit" of Nero.[6] But even my later-date position, that Revelation was composed during the reign of Domitian (81–96 CE), does not lend itself well without manipulative calculation for a line of seven roman emperors.[7] For example, if the city having seven hills is Rome, and the seven heads are kings, not kingdoms (17:9), we might begin the seven emperors with Augustus (27 BC-14 AD), followed by Tiberius (14–37), Gaius (37–41), Claudius (41–54), Nero (54–68), Vespasian (69–79), and Titus (79–81), with Domitian (81–96) being the eighth who "was, and is not, is himself also the eighth, and is of the seven" (Rev 17:11).

The first five (the Julio-Claudian dynasty) have fallen. Transitional emperors Galba (68–69), Otho, and Vitellius (69) without dynasties are discounted. Domitian and Titus are sons of Vespasian; therefore, Domitian "is of the seven, and is going to perdition" (17:11). Note that Julius Caesar is not listed as first before Augustus. Tacitus, considered by modern scholars as one of the greatest Roman historians, appears to have considered Augustus the first Roman emperor. In contrast, Suetonius considers Julius the first Roman emperor.[8] The Suetonius system puts "the one who is" (17:10) as Nero, implying that Revelation was written before 70 AD. Either case is possible, but John seems primarily concerned with the eighth emperor, "the one who was." Hence, we are again left with symbology where John uses "seven kings" to communicate that the full period of Roman rule is

5. Matthews, *Atlas of the Roman World*, 189. Old Istanbul (Constantinople) was built on seven hills, which are not very well known even among that city's inhabitants today. Each hill has historical importance, bearing the footprints of the Roman and Ottoman empires.

6. Rogerson, *Commentary*, 1562.

7. Mounce, *Book of Revelation*, 313–16.

8. Wilson, "Problem of the Domitianic Date," 599.

near completion and coming to an end. We do not have to speculate upon the seven kings and miss the more important point of the entire period of Roman rule and its demand for emperor worship.

In this regard, the woman and the beast from the sea may represent idolatrous Rome (see Rev 13). David L. Mathewson posits, "The exact identity of the beast is not revealed, but in light of chapter 13 it represents the power of Rome and its emperor."[9] However, if one is to conceive the Olivet Discourse in Matt 24; Mark 13; and Luke 21 as a subject of end times, the fate of Rome is not addressed; thus, the beast could represent Jerusalem. In Jer 22:8, Jerusalem is referred to as the "great city." In Rev 11:8, Jerusalem is spiritually called "Sodom and Egypt," which was also a reference to Babylon. John sees "the woman, drunk with the blood of the saints and with the blood of the martyrs of Jesus" (Rev 17:6)—carried forward from "His land and His people" of Jerusalem in Deut 32:43 (see also Rev 18:20, 24).

In addition to Rome and Constantinople, Jerusalem also sat upon seven hills. However, Malinowski writes, "everyone knows that Rome was built on seven hills,"[10] and they are named the Capitoline (Tarpeius), the Palatine (Pallanteum), the Quirinal, the Caelian, the Aventine, the Esquiline, and the Viminal. Malinowski includes the seven kings ruling before Rome became a republic as "1) Romulus, 2) Numa Pompilius, 3) Tullus Hostilius, 4) Ancus Marcius, 5) Tarquinius Priscus, 6) Servius Tullius and 7) Tarquinius Superbus."[11]

The Jews of Jerusalem were also idolatrous. In Rev 17:5, the name "Babylon the Great" written on the woman's forehead, the woman who was arrayed in purple and scarlet, clearly indicates she is the mother of harlots. Chilton writes, "The metaphor of harlotry is exclusively used in the Old Testament for a city or nation that has abandoned the Covenant and turned to false gods."[12] With the two exceptions of Tyre and Nineveh, the term harlotry was used for faithless Israel.[13] A. M. Woods discounts Jerusalem as Babylon and argues that nothing explains how first century

9. Mathewson, *Companion to the Book of Revelation*, 99.

10. Malinowski, "Septimontium," 4.

11. Malinowski, "Septimontium," 3.

12. Chilton, *Days of Vengence,* 468.

13. Pagan cities Tyre (Isa 23:15–17) and Nineveh (Nah 3:4) had once been in covenant with God. See 1 Kgs 5:1–12; 9:13; Amos 1:9; and John 3:5–10.

Jerusalem could be the great city which "reigns over the kings of the earth" (Rev 17:18).[14]

Regarding Rome or Jerusalem as the Great Babylon, Joseph A. Seiss offers a conclusive observation, "On none of the current methods of treating this Book is it possible to come to any clear, consistent, and satisfying conclusions with regard to it."[15] He suggests we must consign the whole subject to the "department of doubt and uncertainty."[16] However, Osborne implies Rome as the Great Babylon in his writing about a coin minted in A.D. 71 depicting the goddess Roma sitting on the seven hills of Rome (17:9) with a sword.[17] Most scholars identify the woman in Rev 17:5–6 as Babylon, The Mother of Harlots, Rome.

Contrasting the unholy trinity (the dragon, the beast of the earth, and the beast of the sea in Rev 12 and 13), the beast having sevens heads and ten horns which the harlot controls has no alliance. The angel explains that the ten horns are ten kings who have received no kingdom yet. The harlot controls these ten kings. These ten kings become of one mind, align themselves with the beast (government/commerce), the war against the Lamb, and eventually turn on the harlot (religiosity/spirituality), just as God has ordained. God will fulfill His purpose. Even during this appalling conflict, God is in control. We are approaching the fall of Babylon, a repeat performance in the next chapter.

In Rev 18:2, we learn of John seeing yet another angel coming down from Heaven with the cry "Babylon the great is fallen, is fallen" as we read previously in Rev 14:8. Additionally, Isaiah prophesied about the fall in Isa 21:9, and Jeremiah tells of it in Jer 50:8. People were repeatedly told to get away from unclean things, to get out of Babylon in Isa 52:11; Jer 51:45; Ezek 20:41; and 2 Cor 6:14, 17. John applies Old Testament stories to new biblical events.[18] The angel highlights that the nations have succumbed to her wrath, and the kings have committed fornication. The merchants of the earth have become rich through the abundance of her luxury (Rev18:3).

---

14. Woods, "Have the Prophecies," 350.

15. Seiss, *Apocalypse*, 385.

16. Seiss, *Apocalypse*, 386.

17. Osborne, *Revelation*, 608.

18. In Revelation, John uses more allusions from the Old Testament books of Isaiah, Daniel, Psalms, Genesis, Deuteronomy, Jeremiah, Joel, and Zechariah than what is used by others in the entire New Testament.

Like the Jezebel in Thyatira, the prostitute rider of the beast seduced people to material and legislative immorality in direct conflict with the spiritual.

The world mourns Babylon's fall when the fires of the one-hour judgment devour all the luxuries and riches once exploited by the merchants of Babylon are no longer available. "The merchants of these things, who became rich by her, will stand at a distance for fear of her torment, weeping and wailing" (Rev 18:15). Mathewson beautifully sums up the judgment of the seventh bowl with "Although Babylon/Rome appears glamorous and invincible, John unveils its true nature: it is corrupt, godless, evil, and guilty of murdering the saints and people on the earth."[19]

When the angel throws the millstone into the sea, it is "Thus with violence the great city Babylon shall be thrown down and shall not be found anymore" (Rev 18:21). In Jer 51:63, Jeremiah prophesied, "Now it shall be when you have finished reading this book, that you shall tie a stone to it and throw it out into the Euphrates. Then you shall say, 'Thus Babylon shall sink and not rise from the catastrophe that I will bring upon her.'"

The fall of Babylon is predicted in Rev 17. Still, destruction is not described until Rev 18, regarding those who "will weep" and how material goods are not available for purchase and how great riches came to nothing in one hour. The judgment of Babylon took one hour! Is this the finality of Babylon? The earth is harvested in Rev 14, bowl judgments were poured out in Rev 16, and the beasts have yet to be destroyed. The final battle and Christ are yet to come. Yet Babylon truly fell when the great millstone was thrown into the sea. The fall of Babylon is not the fall of the world. However, if we view Rev 17 and 18 globally and the concept of Babylon in terms of corrupt world trade, greedy commerce, and selfish monopolization of property, peoples, land, and national treasures, then, the fall of Babylon would contribute to worldwide chaos.

The great harlot was judged, and Rev 19 begins with "Alleluia!" Jubilation proceeds in Heaven when the twenty-four elders and four living creatures fall and worship God, saying Amen! Alleluia! Revelation is the only place in the New Testament that includes the word alleluia (praise the Lord), and the word appears four times. The believers on earth praise and participate in divine worship in Rev 19:6–8. Babylon has fallen, and unlike the fall of Judah, no remnant will survive the fall of Babylon. "Let none of them escape" (Jer 50:29). "The marriage of the Lamb has come" (Rev 19:7)

---

19. Mathewson, *Companion to the Book of Revelation*, 106.

fulfills the commitments expressed earlier in Scripture (Is 54:5–8; Hos 2:19, 20; and Eph 5:26, 27). Christ is on His way!

In Rev 19:9–10, John falls to his feet to worship the one who proclaimed blessings on those called to the marriage supper of the Lamb and the true sayings of God. The angel rebuked John for trying to worship a mere creature, an act of reverence that might tempt anyone witnessing what John beheld.

Chapter Fifteen

# Cycle Six

## The Final Battle (Rev 19:11–19:21)

HEAVEN IS OPENED A fourth time. Unlike the first time when John in the Spirit sees God on His throne (Rev 4:1), John sees a rider, Christ, on a white horse, a symbol of war.[1] This is not to be interpreted as Christ's second coming but rather as Jesus coming in judgment upon the beast (the first beast, the beast of the sea), and the false prophet (the beast of the earth).

Recall that on Palm Sunday, Jesus rode in peace into Jerusalem on a donkey (Matt 21:5). The armies in Heaven follow Jesus, and just as in Rev 1:16, "out of His mouth goes a sharp sword" (Rev 19:15). This heavenly army consists of those who have died in faith. The King of kings and Lord of lords has an angel invite an extensive list of "guests"—those targeted by the sixth seal in Rev 16:15—as dinner for all the birds to devour at the "supper of the great God." This starkly contrasts with the "marriage supper of the Lamb" in Rev 19:8–9.

End of story. There is no real clash in Rev 19. Jesus wins just by speaking. Jesus wins just by showing up. The armies following him are all dressed in white linen of priestly attire, not battle attire.[2] The beast of the sea persecuting the saints (Rev 13:1–10), and the nation-deceiving false prophet (beast of the earth), are "cast alive into the lake of fire and the rest were killed" (Rev 19:20–21). Fire is frequently associated with all-consuming judgment (Is 66:15, 16; Joel 2:3). The beasts become the final Hell's first inhabitants.

1. The second Heaven is opened was in Rev 11:19; the third in 15:5.
2. Johnson, *Discipleship*, 328.

Lusthaus refers to Matt 25:31–46 as perhaps the most important passage for understanding biblical hell; a fiery location where the wicked will go away into everlasting punishment.[3] If their annihilation is not the dissolution of one final antichrist, their termination is certainly representative of the evil world system. The beasts and his armies are defeated.

3. Lusthaus, "History of Hell," 178.

# Chapter Sixteen

# Cycle Seven

## The Reign of the Saints and the Last Judgment
### (Rev 20:1–21:8)

REVELATION 20 IS ONE of the great chapters of the Bible. For Reverend Dr. Philip Schuiling, it is his litmus test for commentaries on Revelation.[1] I plan to journey through Rev 20 roughly verse-by-verse.

At the end of chapter 19, Christ strikes the nations with his sharp sword, rules them with an iron rod, and treads the winepress. The beast and the false prophet are cast into the lake of fire, the rest are killed, and the birds have plenty to devour. Revelation 20 picks up with a mere angel, an angel "jailer" coming down from Heaven with keys to lock away and seal "the dragon, the serpent of old, who is the Devil and Satin" for a thousand years (Rev 20:2). In the concept of "binding the strong man," Jesus demonstrated his defeat of Satan in Matt 12:26–29; Mark 3:26–27; and Luke 11:20–23. Satan is powerless to prevent the coming of the kingdom.

Although Christ's initial earthly ministry did not bind Satan, "Your adversary the devil walks around like a roaring lion" (1 Pet 5:8), the binding of Satan began during the earthly ministry of Jesus. "If Satan casts out Satan, he is divided against himself" (Matt 26:26–29). The fact that Christ uses a single angel to incapacitate Satan displays Christ's immeasurable power compared to Satan's. Satan is rendered completely inactive by being locked away and sealed. Premillennialists would claim this as the second

---

1. See his endorsement for this book.

coming, but Satan is not permanently bound because he is later released in Rev 20:7. Revelation 20:1–3 refers to events just before the thousand years.

During those thousand years, John catches a glance at some thrones and then notices they are occupied by the headless, stoned, and otherwise butchered souls, and judgment was committed to them, who perished for their witness to Jesus and the word of God. "A judgment was made in favor of the saints of the Most High" (Dan 7:22) because just as we shall see that there are degrees of punishment, there are also degrees of reward. "And every transgression and disobedience received a just reward" (Heb 2:2). The stage is set with these souls, and only these souls, who get to live and reign with Christ for a thousand years. Revelation 20:4–6 refers to the millennium itself. "The rest of the dead did not live again until the thousand years were finished" (Rev 20:5). These souls are the martyred saints John saw under the altar when Christ opened the fifth seal.[2] "This is the first resurrection"(Rev 20:5) within the context of this section of Revelation.[3] Christ was the very first resurrection (1 Cor 15:20).

However, one commentator,[4] and some others, write that the first resurrection of these souls, the martyred saints of Rev 20:4, was when they were slain at the hands of their persecutors and not when John saw them as "the souls of those who had been beheaded for their witness to Jesus and for the word of God" (Rev 20:4). This is a rationalism or empty concept fallacy or simply a stretch with too much extrapolation of Scripture. Revelation 20:5 clearly states, "This is the first resurrection." Dr. Johnson writes, "death ushered them into the presence of God, where they now worship as priests and reign as kings." His reference of Rev 7:9–12 alluding to the "ones in white robes" as those martyred falls two verses short of the explanation in Rev 7:14, where they are the "ones who come out of the great tribulation and washed their robes and made them white in the blood of the Lamb."

The great tribulation can be seen as the final period of persecution shortly before the second coming. Tribulation for Christians occurs throughout the church age; it is not reserved just for the martyred. "All who

2. These are the souls John saw under the altar of those who had been slain for the word of God and for the testimony they held (Rev 6:9).

3. Clear predictions of resurrection are evident in Scripture. For example, Matt 27:52, "and the graves were opened; and many bodies of the saints who had fallen asleep were raised; and coming out of the graves after His resurrection, they went into the holy city and appeared to many." Dan 12:2, "And many of those who sleep in the dust of the earth shall awake, Some to everlasting life, Some to shame *and* everlasting contempt."

4. Johnson, "Last Things, Systematic Theology," 37.

desire to live godly in Christ Jesus will suffer persecution" (2 Tim 3:12; also see 2 Thess 1:5–6).

My point is that we have the saints, all the saints,[5] including the non-martyred faithful Christians, and Christ together for one-thousand years while Satan is bound in the bottomless pit for that same duration (Rev 20:3). John does not explicitly present other than martyred saints, but he does state, "Blessed and holy is he who has part in the first resurrection. Over such the second death has no power. . ." (Rev 20:6, emphasis added) and only the saints who overcome the tribulation (which include the non-martyred) will experience the absence of the second death (Rev 2:11). This "second death" is the eternal judgment that awaits all whose names are not written in the Book of Life (Rev 20:14–15). In addition, the "tribulation saints" also include the Old Testament saints, first mentioned in Ps. 50:1–6. Therefore, the first resurrected are seen by John following his glimpse of the thrones.

These "one-thousand years" should be a perfect time for humans to willingly serve God in a seemingly perfect environment, especially if we view this time as coinciding with the church age. The first resurrection involves every righteous one who believes in Christ. The resurrection of the righteous dead is separated from the resurrection of the wicked dead by a thousand years. Practically all instances of resurrection are bodily resurrections, not spiritual. John likely saw the souls in Rev 6:9, and 20:4 in a similar manner as the three thousand souls baptized in Acts 2:41 or the souls looked after by the leaders in Hebrew 13:17. This first resurrection is genuine as the resurrection of the body of Matt 27:52.

This thousand-year, long period of time, is the first time in all human history in which Satan is limited (bound) in executing his work of deception. But humans will respond according to prophesy, "The heart is deceitful above all things, And desperately wicked; Who can know it?" (Jer 17:9), and all will not appreciate this otherwise one-thousand years (or the metaphor for a long period of time) of perfect environment.

5. This means all of the saints and not of any nationality (Jew, Israel, etc.) confirmed in Rev 5:9, "For You were slain, And have redeemed us to God by Your blood. Out of every tribe and tongue and people and nation." We are members together of one body. Also, in Eph 3:6, "that the Gentiles should be fellow heirs, of the same body, and partakers of His promise in Christ through the gospel." First Peter 2:9, "But you *are* a chosen generation, a royal priesthood, a holy nation, His own special people, that you may proclaim the praises of him who called you out of darkness into His marvelous light."

Revelation 20:7–10 refer to events occurring at the end of the thousand years. At the end of the thousand years, Satan is released "for a little while" in a doomed effort to deceive the nations and gather the final human enemies of God, named Gog and Magog, eliciting the time when Gog, of the land of Magog lead one last assault on the people of Israel (Ezek 38–39). Not to be identified as specific nations, Gog and Magog, "surrounded the camp of the saints and the beloved city" (Rev 20:9). This is the battle of Armageddon, and it takes on cosmic and mythical proportions not necessarily confined to *har Megiddo,* the city in the Jezreel Valley.

What nations remain for Satan to deceive? In Rev 19:15, Christ strikes the nations with His sharp sword and rules them with a rod of iron. In Rev 19:18, the birds devoured the "flesh of all people, free and slave, both small and great." Who remains but the righteous? One answer is that Rev 20 does not follow Rev 19 chronologically. Another may be that Revelation has a cyclical structure where the same things are looked at repeatedly but from different perspectives. Perhaps during the thousand years in a "perfect environment," the righteous made descendants (Isa 65:18–25). The descendants of the righteous who are born during this time have their sinful Adamic nature and need salvation, many of which become victims of Satan's wiles. Satan is bound, but sin yet continues.

The enemies of God are as numerous "as the sand of the sea" (20:8). Satan serves to reveal once more his incurable bent toward evil.[6] But fire came down from God out of Heaven (a frequent method of divine judgment on earth)[7] and devoured them, and the devil was cast into the lake of fire. Satan's judgment is finally executed. As in Gen 3:15, the heel is bruised. The enmity God placed between his seed and her seed and the consequent division of human community between the redeemed, who love God, and the reprobate, who love self, is over. There is no sanctifying grace or annihilation for fallen angels, just eternal punishment.

We enter the great white throne room of Rev 20:11. There are seven throne room scenes carried out in the book of Revelation.[8] The seventh throne room is the Great White Throne Judgment.

> Then I saw a great white throne and him who sat on it, from whose
> face the earth and the heaven fled away. And there was found no

6. Thomas, *Revelation,* 423.

7. Cf. Gen 19:24; Exod 9:23–24; Lev 9:24; 10:2; Num 11:1; 16:35; 26:10; 1 Kgs 18:38; 2 Kgs 1:10, 12, 14; 1 Chr 21:26; 2 Chr 7:1, 3; Ps 11:6; etc.

8. Rev 4:1—5:14; 7:9–17; 8:1–4; 11:15–18; 16:10; 19:4–5; and 20:11–15.

> place for them. And I saw the dead, small and great, standing before God, and books were opened. And another book was opened, which is the Book of Life. And the dead were judged according to their works, by the things which were written in the books. The sea gave up the dead who were in it, and Death and Hades delivered up the dead who were in them. And they were judged, each one according to his works. Then Death and Hades were cast into the lake of fire. This is the second death. And anyone not found written in the Book of Life was cast into the lake of fire.

God saw that "the earth and Heaven fled away."[9] This begins the final judgment. The first resurrection, a thousand years earlier, was made clear. Now the second resurrection is implied when John "saw the dead, small and great, standing before God (this points to the resurrection even of unbelievers) and "the books were opened" (Rev 20:12). In Jewish apocalyptic visions, the plural term "books" symbolizes God's judgment[10] against the sins of the wicked (Dan 7: 9–12). After we die once, judgment comes (Heb 9:27). The books were opened followed by another book, the Book of Life, and judgment was made according to works (2 Cor 5:10; Matt 16:27; John 5:28–29; Gal 6:7–9; Rev 20:13; 22:12). We are saved by grace through faith and not by works (Eph 2:8–9). However, faith without works is dead (Jas 2:14–26). Nowhere in Scripture does it say that God will judge faith alone. Christians will stand before Christ on the day of judgment to receive "according to what he has done, good or bad" (2 Cor 5:10). Whoever was not in the Book of Life was cast into the lake of fire.

We are not told how many books were opened for each person, but we are told in Rev 20:13 that each person was judged according to his works. There are degrees of punishment. There is no degree of reward in this judgment because the righteous were previously judged before the thrones at the first resurrection. This is the resurrection of the evil dead after the thousand years. Scripture overwhelmingly suggests that in this judgment there will be degrees of punishment according to works.

The following are a few examples: "Truly, I say to you, it will be more bearable on the day of judgment for the land of Sodom and Gomorrah than for that town" (Matt 10:15). "But I tell you, it will be more bearable on the day of judgment for Tyre and Sidon than for you . . . But I tell you that it will be more tolerable on the day of judgment for the land of Sodom than

---

9. But not to worry, John sees a new heaven and a new earth in the next chapter!

10. Rogerson, *Commentary*, 1568.

for you" (Matt 11:22, 24). "I tell you, on the day of judgment people will give account for every careless word they speak, for by your words you will be justified, and by your words you will be condemned" (Matt 12:36–37). "And that servant who knew his master's will but did not get ready or act according to his will, will receive a severe beating. But the one who did not know, and did what deserved a beating, will receive a light beating. Everyone to whom much was given, of him much will be required, and from him to whom they entrusted much, they will demand the more" (Luke 12:47–48). "But because of your hard and impenitent heart you are storing up wrath for yourself on the day of wrath when God's righteous judgment will be revealed" (Rom 2:5). "How much worse punishment, do you think, will be deserved by the one who has trampled underfoot the Son of God, and has profaned the blood of the covenant by which he was sanctified, and has outraged the Spirit of grace?" (Heb 10:29).

The many examples in Scripture give us a clearer picture of judgment according to works. But let us not miss the point of this judgment. The determining factor regarding one's presence in Heaven or Hell is not works but whether one's name is in the Book of Life (Rev 20:15). The reprobate dead are all being sent to the same address, and they will all experience misery. We gather from the Bible that those in the lake of fire are expected to suffer untold, unimaginable horror, especially for humans, because the everlasting fire was prepared for the devil and his angels (Matt 25:41).

The sea gives up the dead who did not die a physical death or perhaps were cremated or otherwise disintegrated. Death and Hades joined the physical bodies with the spirits of the unsaved.[11] "Anyone not found written in the Book of Life was cast into the lake of fire" in their resurrected, indestructible bodies (Rev 20:15). This is the second death. We have yet to reach the climax of this series.

In Rev 21:1, John sees a new heaven and a new earth, not a renovated earth and heaven but transfigured new! Like a bride adorned for her husband. The image is traditional, and perhaps one God's people would have imagined when they returned to Jerusalem after being exiled in Babylon.[12] The next rung in the rising action of this climactic ladder is that there is no sea! Most of our current earth's surface is covered with water, but the new earth does not come with a sea. The new earth tabernacle of God is with men and is not tangible; also missing are tears, death, sorrow, crying, and

---

11. Zuck, *Bible Knowledge*, 983.

12. See Isa 49:18; 52:1; and 61:10.

pain. It is a transfiguration of the old earth, as indicated in Isa 65:17–25 and Rom 8:21–23. God tells John to make a record because every word is true and faithful, another testimony of historical fact and present reality for all who believe. As the Alpha and the Omega, the Beginning and the End, God Almighty will freely give the water of life to him who thirsts and a lake of fire to the unbelieving. Revelation 21:6 is the second time God speaks directly to John, the first being in Rev 1:8 with the other bookend of, "I am the Alpha and the Omega." Again, the targeted message is "he who overcomes shall inherit all things" (Rev 21:7).

Just as in our resurrection, our bodies are transfigured, "God gives it a body as He pleases, and to each seed its own body" (1 Cor 15:38), and "The body is sown in corruption, it is raised in incorruption. It is sown in dishonor; it is raised in glory. It is sown in weakness; it is raised in power. It is sown a natural body; it is raised a spiritual body. There is a natural body, and there is a spiritual body" (1 Cor 15:42–44). This may be one of the reasons the new earth is without a sea. The sea is constantly changing, and one might argue that it is, therefore, not always the same, it is just another sea, whereas the new earth is not another earth but a new earth. I think John described everything he saw and heard throughout Revelation using language he understood as the Lord provided. John could only use a vocabulary connected to his life at that time. The sea is viewed as a seething cauldron,[13] never permanent, and it is up from where the beast comes (Rev 13:1). Finally, "The wicked are like the troubled sea, When it cannot rest, Whose waters cast up mire and dirt" (Isa 57:20). As we will soon read, the sea is one of seven evils John speaks of being no more.

In apocalyptic literature, the sea is the abode of death, sin, and evil. In the New Jerusalem, there is no evil, therefore, no sea. God "will give of the fountain of the water of life freely to him who thirsts. He who overcomes shall inherit all things, and I will be his God and he shall be My son" (Rev 21:6–7). The Alpha and the Omega, the Beginning and the End has declared "It is done" and among the missing sea are the cowards, unbelievers, abominable, murders, sexual immoral, sorcerers, idolaters, and liars because they are in the lake of fire.

13. Morris, *Revelation*, 232.

# Section IV—THE NEW JERUSALEM (Rev 21:9–22:5)

JOHN FIRST SAW NEW Jerusalem in 21:2, but he sees it again, the holy Jerusalem, to be distinguished from the earlier Jerusalem, descending out of Heaven from God (Rev 21:10). To the angel of the church in Philadelphia John wrote about the new Jerusalem (Rev 3:12). In Rev 17:3, one of the seven angels who had the seven bowls took John *in the Spirit* to see the prostitute, the harlot on the beast representing the Roman Empire. In Rev 21:9, one of the seven angels, who may or may not be the same angel as in Rev 17:3, carried John *in the Spirit* to see details of the Bride, the wife of the Lamb. The other two visions where John is carried *in the Spirit* were in Rev 1:10 and 4:2. New Jerusalem is a city, the Bride, the wife of the Lamb, and the bride of Christ is the community of Saints—the church (Eph 5:25–33; Rev 19:1–8).

Consider the new Jerusalem as a symbolic representation of the church triumphant.[1] It was the temple that gave glory to the earthy Jerusalem; the Lamb of God is the sacred element in New Jerusalem.[2] New Jerusalem, a great city, is a perfect cube, like the Holy of Holies in the temple (1 Kgs 6:20). Still, instead of the old dimension of 20 cubits (30 feet) wide, the dimension of the new is twelve thousand furlongs, about 1400 miles cubed. The angel also measured the wall at 144 cubits (twelve times twelve) or about 216 feet.[3] John records the wall as "great and high," not great and thick. If we wonder if the wall is 216 feet high or 216 feet thick, we miss the symbolic meaning of "twelve." Like the twelve precious stones

1. Sproul, "New Jerusalem," 10.

2. Sproul, "New Jerusalem," 11.

3. Wilcock, *Message of Revelation*, 208.

on the high priest's breastplate (Exod 28:17–20; 39:10–13), the foundations of the wall had the names of the twelve apostles and on the twelve gates were the names of the twelve tribes of the children of Israel. According to Miller-Naude, "The list of precious stones as the foundation of the New Jerusalem is clearly based upon the LXX list of the precious stones of the high priest."[4] Twelve, in this context, designates the whole people of God. The city is then measured as the temple was in Rev 11:1 to show no doubt that every inch is accounted for and known to God. The measuring reveals a shape quite odd enough to enable us to accept the oddity of the jewel-like lamp of Rev 21:11. These figures are necessarily human or angelic measurements (v.17) because they expressed in human terms things which are in fact, spiritual or more accurately multidimensional and therefore incapable of actual computation as we would understand it. In other words, the dimensions of the city are symbolic and not to be taken literally. Imagine 1400 miles cubed!

The walls of the new Jerusalem have twelve continuously open gates inscribed with the twelve names of the tribes of Israel and twelve foundations bearing the names of the twelve apostles (Rev 21:12–14). What matters is that Revelation presents glorious imagery that ultimately reflects our heavenly home for all believers from both the old and new covenants as the church victorious.[5] John speaks of the church in exalted terms, and the extensive description is found in Rev 21:9–21.

In the glory of the New Jerusalem, there is no sea in the new earth, and there is no temple, sun, or moon in New Jerusalem. The glory of God illuminates entirely, and some expositors surmise, therefore, there are likely no stars either. On this and similar "mysteries," one is wise to heed the warning of Rev 22:18–19 against adding to Scripture. We humbly shrug, tilt our head, and rest on the assurance that Jesus is the light of the world (John 8:12). "There shall by no means enter it anything that defiles, or causes an abomination or a lie, but only those who are written in the Lamb's Book of Life" (Rev 21:27). Alteration is an attempt to deny God's authority and wisdom, places our way above God's way, and is a blatant expression of unbelief and arrogance.

God's presence pervades every aspect, there is no need for a temple. Our body is the temple of the Holy Spirit, and believers have no need for an earthly temple (1 Cor 6:19–20). The only inhabitants of the New Earth

---

4. Miller-Naudé and Naudé, "Textual Interrelationships," 14.

5. Gentry, "New Creation," 120.

are those whose names were found in the Book of Life. There will be no possibility of desecration, like a deceiving serpent anywhere (Rev 21:27). No unclean thing will ever enter the city. Were Jesus to restore creation merely to its original state in Eden, we would have to be on the lookout for the serpent, for he tempted Adam and Eve in the garden (Gen 3). This is not the case for the New Earth.

The angel of the seven plagues shows John in Rev 22:1, the "pure river of water of life" running crystal clear down the middle of the street from the throne of God. God resides in all of New Jerusalem, and this miraculous river, foretold by Joel, Ezekiel, and Zechariah,[6] flows through the length of Scripture[7] from the Old Testament saints (Ps. 1:1–3; Je.17:7, 8) to John 4:14, "but whoever drinks of the water that I shall give him will never thirst. But the water that I shall give him will become in him a fountain of water springing up into everlasting life." And from John 7:37, 38, "If anyone thirsts, let him come to Me and drink. He who believes in Me, as the Scripture has said, out of his heart will flow rivers of living water."

Revelation somewhat parallels Gen. In Genesis, we learn of creation; in Revelation, we learn of the new earth and New Jerusalem. In Gen 1:20, "Then God said, "Let the waters abound with an abundance of living creatures, and let birds fly above the earth across the face of the firmament of the heavens." In Rev 7:17, " for the Lamb who is in the midst of the throne will shepherd them and lead them to living fountains of waters." The Garden of Eden pales compared to the Garden City we will have with Christ's second coming. "In the middle of its street, and on either side of the river, was the tree of life (Rev 22:2) and in Gen 2:9, "And out of the ground the Lord God made every tree grow that is pleasant to the sight and good for food." The tree of life was also in the midst of the garden, and the tree of the knowledge of good and evil. Earlier in Revelation, "And out of the ground the Lord God made every tree grow that is pleasant to the sight and good for food. The tree of life was also in the midst of the garden, and the tree of the knowledge of good and evil" (Rev 2:7). These trees bear fruit twelve months out of the year and the leaves are for healing the nations. These are powerful trees!

Access to God's life-giving blessings, the tree of life once barred, is now available. Gone is the flaming sword that kept man from the "tree of

---

6. Joel before the exile (Joel 3:18), Ezekiel during it (Ezek 47:1–9), and Zechariah after it (Zech 14:8).

7. Wilcock, *Message of Revelation,* 211.

life" in the Garden of Eden. Those who are judged as righteous are sent to Heaven, where they are now permitted access to the tree of life, and all God has to offer. The trees of life and the river of life reflect the permanent fullness of life to come in the new creation. The new Jerusalem and the new creation fulfill the hope of every person of God.

Ready or not, Jesus is coming and coming quickly. "In a moment, in the twinkling of an eye, at the last trumpet. For the trumpet will sound, and the dead will be raised incorruptible, and shall be changed" (1 Cor 15:52).

The closing benediction brings us back to the gospel's message, the gift of His grace, "The grace of our Lord Jesus Christ be with you all. Amen" (Rev 22:21).

# Section V—FINAL EXHORTATIONS
## (Rev 22:6–20)

In Rev 22:8, we read about John falling again to worship before the feet of the angel. This happens after John sees and hears, "Behold, I am coming quickly!" in the previous verse. Scripture reads as if "Behold, I am coming quickly!" was said by the angel. Earlier in Rev 3:11 and 16:15, "I am coming" is clearly by the Lord, as we will soon read in Rev 22:12. The message is truly from God, mediated through the angel, because the angel who represents him commands John to worship the Lord alone (Rev 22:8–9). Throughout some passages of Revelation, we may contemplate who is speaking precisely, but the reality is that every word and every message is inspired and put forth by God. "These words are faithful and true" (Rev 22:6). The angel's purpose "to show" God's message to the prophets overlaps with that attributed to Christ, who mediates John's opening vision of heavenly worship as in Rev 4:1, for instance.[1]

In contrast to Dan 12:4, "Seal the book until the time of the end," John is told by the angel, "Do not seal the words of the prophecy of this book, for the time is at hand" (Rev 22:10). Daniel is told, "for the words are closed up and sealed till the time of the end" (Dan 12:9) whereas John is told, "for the time is at hand," like Rev 1:3. Daniel is hundreds of years before the cross; John is less than a century after. John's message must be published and kept (Dan 8:26; 12:4). Jesus emphasizes this with words of recompense and somewhat parallel to the "dead, small and great, standing before God" (Rev 20:12). The Book of Life is the heavenly roster of those destined for new life through the purchase of Christ's blood. This "precept" is mentioned throughout Scripture and early in Rev 3:5 and 5:9. In this final era,

---

1. Rogerson, *Commentary*, 1570.

Jesus and his gospel form a dividing line between the unrighteous and the righteous. People must decide to follow him or become more confirmed in their evil (Rev 22:11).

It might be tempting to interpret from Rev 22:14 that it is good alone, "those who do His commandments" that gives the right to the tree of life and entry through the gates into the city. There needs to be more than good alone. Revelation 7:14 reads that those who do His commandments are "the ones who come out of the great tribulation and washed their robes and made them white in the blood of the Lamb." The dogs and sorcerers, the sexually immoral, the murderers, the idolaters, and those who love to lie, are laundry lists of those excluded from the city's gates, the congregation, and anything else otherwise excluded from the blessings of those who follow God's commandments. Again, in Rev 21:27, nothing enters the gate if it defiles or causes abomination. It is reminiscent of the lost in Babylon and raises the awareness level as an exhortation to the hearers.

Dogs and swine are considered unclean in Jewish tradition. Dogs refer to cultic prostitution as noted in Deut 23:18, which addresses various laws, campsite cleanliness, and exclusion.[2] "You shall not bring the wages of a harlot or the price of a dog to the house of the Lord your God for any vowed offering, for both of these are an abomination to the Lord your God" (Deut 23:18). Perhaps in Jewish thought "dogs" lead the list of defilement, "But it has happened to them according to the true proverb: 'A dog returns to his own vomit,' and, 'a sow, having washed, to her wallowing in the mire'" (2 Pet 2:22). "Dog" is a metaphor for something unclean or impure and is in view of the language and culture of the time. We must not make hasty plans to rid our homes of man's best friend.[3]

2. Rogerson, *Commentary,* 1571.

3. "Dogs" represent male prostitutes (Deut 23:18), gentiles (Matt 15:26), and Judaizers (Phil 3:2–3). See also: 2 Kgs 8:13; Ps 22:16; 22:20; Isa 56:10; Matt 7:6; and Mark 7:27.

# Section VI—CLOSING BLESSING
## (Rev 22:21)

THE ENDING OF REVELATION closes similarly to many church services—with an altar call. Jesus tells us, "Come!" Jesus reminds us that He is the Root and the Offspring of David, the Bright and Morning Star, which is the promise given to the one who overcomes in the church of Thyatira, Rev 2:28. John writes, "Come, Lord Jesus!" We recognize that His coming, Him as the Morning Star, will mark the dawn of a new day. John seeks to protect the Revelation prophesy and underscores his authority with a warning to everyone who hears with a two-fold curse: tamper with this book, and God will add to the plagues; take away from this book, and God will take away one's part from the Book of Life.

The Christian hope lies in four things that Jesus-through-John provides in the blessedness of Revelation's message. First, Jesus is the ruler of the kings on earth (Rev 1:5). Under God's sovereign rule, we know that whatever happens on earth is according to His sovereign purpose. Nothing and no thing is more powerful than God. Second, Jesus loves us, and nothing we experience in this life will negate the love of Christ (Rom 8:31–39). Third, Jesus freed us from our sins by His atoning blood, "Therefore if the Son makes you free, you shall be free indeed" (Jn. 8:36). Fourth, we are a kingdom of priests to God and Father. "He has delivered us from the power of darkness and conveyed us into the kingdom of the Son of His love" (Col 1:13).

# Epilogue

THE TIME IS NEAR—BUT not without warning. Now, but not yet. In Rev 1:3, we find the time is near as well as in Rev 22:10. Revelation is by Jesus Christ from Jesus Christ, the One who knows the last day, and through which John has graciously given us all the indicators. Throughout Revelation, things are not what they seem. There is more to reality than we can know with our limited comprehension, intellect, and emotions.

When my mother was several days from her death, she said some strange things that boggled my mind regarding death. Convinced she was that, on occasion, she could see dead people. To my question, did she recognize them? She said no. On another occasion, she claimed a visitor would come to see her. This visitor would be the most unlikely of any visitor to darken my doorway. Yet two days later, this visitor came. My mother knew the visitor well, and both enjoyed the occasion. There is so much we do not understand or comprehend about death, life, and the afterlife. We must always be open for God's glory to prevail.

We are continually trying to figure out life. There are things we want to know, some things we should know, and some things we are not to know. Nothing around us tells us the very end of times, but every decay around us tells us the end is near. We must always be mindful that the time is close. Jesus will return. The last trumpet will sound with a warning.

# Bibliography

Alcorn, Randy. *Heaven.* Carol Stream, IL: Tyndale, 2004.

Allmand, Christopher. "Particular Uses of the De Re Militari." In *The De Re Militari of Vegetius: The Reception, Transmission and Legacy of a Roman Text in the Middle Ages,* 83–147. Cambridge, UK: Cambridge University Press, 2011.

Arand, Charles P. "Antichrist? The Lutheran Confessions on the Papacy." *Concordia Journal* 29, no. 4 (2003) 392–406.

Ascough, Richard S. *Religious Rivalries and the Struggle for Success in Sardis and Smyrna.* Waterloo, Ontario: Wilfrid Laurier University Press, 2005.

Böttrich, Christfried. "The Angel of Tartarus and the Supposed Coptic Fragments of 2 Enoch." *Early Christianity* 4, no. 4 (2013) 509–21.

Barclay, William. *Letters to the Seven Churches.* London: SCM Press Limited, 1957.

Barry, J. D., and L. Wentz, eds. *Lexham Bible Dictionary.* Bellingham, WA: Lexham, 2016.

Bauckham, R. J. *The Climax of Prophesy: Studies on the Book of Revelation.* Edinburgh: T. & T. Clark, 1993.

Beasley-Murray, G. R. *The Book of Revelation.* Eugene, OR: Wipf & Stock, 2010.

Bener, Mustafa. "Modeling and Optimizing of Microwave-Assisted Extraction of Antitoxidants and Phenolics from Wormwood (Artemisia Absinthium L.) Using Response Surface Methodology." *Journal of the Institute of Science & Technology/Fen Bilimleri Estitüsü Dergisi* 10, no. 1 (2020) 357–67.

Bigalke, Ron J., Jr. "The Revival of Futurist Interpretation Following the Reformation." *Journal of Dispensational Theology* 13, no. 38 (2009) 43–56.

Biguzzi, Giancarlo. "Is the Babylon of Revelation Rome or Jerusalem?" *Biblica* 87, no. 3 (2006) 371–86.

Blackwell, Ben C., et al. *Reading Revelation in Context: John's Apocalypse and Second Temple Judaism.* Grand Rapids, MI: Harper Collins, 2019.

Blomberg, Craig L. *A Case for Historic Premillenialism: An Alternative to Left Behind Eschatology.* Grand Rapids, MI: Baker Academic, 2009.

Bousset, W. *Die Offenbarung Johannis.* Gottingen: Vanderhoeck & Ruprecht, 1906.

Bruce, F. F. *New Testament History.* Garden City, NY: Doubleday, 1971.

Buck, Lawrence P. "Anatomia Antichristi." *Sixteenth Century Journal* 42, no. 2 (2011) 349–68.

Camile, Alice. "The Final Battle." *U. S. Catholic* 81, no. 6 (2016) 47–49.

Campbell, Phillip. *The Story of Civilization: Volume I—The Ancient World.* Ashland, OH: TAN Books, 2016.

Cline, Eric H. *Digging Up Armageddon: The Search for the Lost City of Solomon.* Princeton, NJ: Princeton University Press, 2020.

———. *The Battles of Armageddon: Megiddo and the Jezreel Valley from the Bronze Age to the Nuclear Age.* Ann Arbor, MI: The University of Michigan Press, 2000.

Cornell, Tim, and John Matthews. *Atlas of the Roman World.* Oxfordshire: Andromeda Oxford Limited, 1982.

Cory, Catherine A. *The Book of Revelation.* Collegeville, MN: Liturgical, 2006.

Croteau, David A. *Urban Legends of the New Testament: 40 Common Misconceptions.* Nashville, TN: B & H Publishing Group, 2015.

Davis, Dale Ralph. "Relationship between the Seals, Trumpets, and Bowls in the Book of Revelation." *Journal of the Evangelical Theological Society* 16, no. 3 (1973) 149–58.

Dean, R. L. "Chronological Issues in the Book of Revelation." *Bibliotheca Sacra* 160, no. 670 (2011) 217–26.

Decock, Paul B. "The Symbol of Blood in the Apocalypse of John." *Neotestamentica* 38, no. 2 (2004) 157–82.

De Waal, Kayle B. "Two Witnesses and the Land Beast in the Book of Revelation." *Andrews University Seminary Studies* 53, no. 1 (2015) 159–74.

Dunn, James D. G., and John W. Rogerson. *Eerdmans Commentary on the Bible.* Grand Rapids: Eerdmans, 2003.

Ebeling, Jennie. "Engendering the Israelite Harvests." *Near Eastern Archaeology* 79, no. 3 (2016) 186–94.

Elwell, W. A. *Evangelical Commentary on the Bible.* Vol. 3. Grand Rapids, MI: Baker, 1995.

Elwell, W. A., and B. J. Blackwell. *Baker Encyclopedia of the Bible.* Grand Rapids: Baker, 1988.

Ephesus.us. *St. Paul in Ephesus.* https://www.ephesus.us/ephesus/st_paul_in_ephesus.htm.

Espinoza, B. D. *The Lexham Bible Dictionary.* Bellingham, WA: Lexham, 2016.

Eusebius. *The Ecclesiastical History Vols 1–2, Kirsopp Lake, Trans.* Vols. 1–2. Cambridge , MA: Harvard University Press, 1980.

Fastiggi, Robert L. "The Contributions of the Council of Trent to the Catholic Church." *Perichoresis* 18, no. 6 (2020) 3–20.

Fee, Gordon D. *Revelation: A New Covenant Commentary.* Cambridge, MA: Lutterworth, 2013.

Fishman-Duker, Rivkah. *Jerusalem Center for Public Affairs.* November 3, 2019. https://jcpa.org/the-cyrus-debate-ironically-confirms-the-truth-of-jewish-history-in-jerusalem/.

Kaiser, Walter C., Jr., and Duane Garrett. *The Archaeological Study Bible.* Grand Rapids: Zondervan, 2005.

Gentry, Kenneth. "The New Creation." *Tabletalk*, March 1, 2004.

———. *The Book of Revelation Made Easy.* Powder Springs, GA: American Vision, 2008.

Gorman, Michael J. *Reading Revelation Responsibly: Uncivil Worship and Witness: Following the Lamb into the New Creation.* Eugene, OR: Wipf & Stock, 2011.

Gregg, Steve. *Revelation—Four Views, Revised and Updated. A Parallel Commentary.* Nashville, TN: Thomas Nelson, 2013.

Grudem, Wayne. "He Did Not Descend into Hell: A Plea for Following Scripture Instead of The Apostles' Creed." *Journal of the Evangelical Theological Society* 34, no. 1 (1991) 103–113.

Harris, Gregory H. "The Wound of the Beast in the Tribulation." *Bibliotheca Sacra* 156, no. 624 (1999) 459–68.

Hill, C. E. "Hades of Hippolytus or Tartarus of Tertullian: The Authorship of the Fragment De Universo." *Vigiliae Christianae* 43, no. 2 (1989) 105–26.

Horton, Michael. *The Christian Faith, A Systematic Theology for Pilgrims on the Way.* Grand Rapids: Zondervan, 2011.

Huber, Lynn R. "Sexually Explicit? Re–Reading Revelation's 144,000 Virgins as a Response to Roman Discourses." *Journal of Men, Masculinities & Spirituality* 2, no. 1 (2008) 3–28.

Hunter, James Davison. "The Cultural Economy of American Christianity." In *To Change the World: The Irony, Tragedy, and Possibility of Christianity Today,* 79–52. Oxford: Oxford University Press, 2010.

Hutson, Christopher. *First and Second Timothy and Titus.* Grand Rapids, MI: Baker Academic, 2019.

Jacob, Joseph, and Wilhelm Nowack. "Sackcloth." *Jewish Encyclopedia.* 1906. http://www.jewishencyclopedia.com/articles/12981-sackcloth.

Jeremiah, David. *When Christ Appears: An Inspirational Experience Through Revelation.* Franklin: Worthy, 2017.

Johnson, Alan F. *The Expositor's Bible Commentary.* Edited by Frank E. Gaebelein. Vol. 12. Grand Rapids: Zondervan, 1981.

Johnson, Darrell W. *Discipleship on the Edge: An Expository Journey Through the Book of Revelation.* Vancouver: Regent College, 2004.

Johnson, Dennis. "Last Things, Systematic Theology." *Tabletalk,* December 1, 2013.

Jones, Brian W. *The Emperor Domitian.* New York: Routledge, 1992.

Josephus, Flavius. *The Works of Flavius Josephus.* Edited by William Whiston. Philadelphia: London, 1737.

Krodel, Gerhard. *Revelation.* Ontario, Canada: Parasource Marketing, 1989.

Lawrence, David J. "Medieval Refinements in Augustinian Theology: Scholastic Foundations for the Reformation." *Fides et Historia* 33, no. 2 (2001) 53–62.

Lawson, Steven. *Foundations of Grace.* Orlando, FL: Reformation Trust, 2006.

———. *The Moment of Truth.* Sanford, FL: Reformation Trust, 2018.

Leithart, Peter. "Laodicean Water." *Patheos.* November 11, 2016. https//www.patheos.com/blogs/leithart/2016/10/laodicean-water/.

Leon, Noe. *The Seven Spirits of God.* Holladay, UT: Merkur, 2013.

Loasby, Roland E. "'Har-Magedon' According to the Hebrew in the Setting of the Seven Last Plagues of Revelation 16." *Andrews University Seminary Studies* 27, no. 2 (1989) 129–32.

Lusthaus, Jonathan. "A History of Hell: The Jewish Origins of the Idea of Gehenna in the Gospels of Matthew and Mark." *Journal for the Academic Study of Religion* 21, no. 2 (2008) 175–87.

Magnusson, Magnus. "Travel Guide Valley of Armegeddon." *American Israel Tours,* 2020. https://www.americaisraeltours.com/israel–travel–guide/tiberias–galilee/visit–tiberias–galilee/valley–of–armageddon.

Malinowski, Gosciwit. "Septimontium (Seven Hills) as Condito Sine qua Non for a City to Pretend to Be a Capital." *Horizons: Seoul Journal of Humanities* 8, no. 1 (2017) 3–26.

Mark, Joshua J. "Babylon." https://www.ancient.eu/babylon/.

Mathewson, David L. *A Companion to the Book of Revelation.* Eugene, OR: Cascade, 2020.

Mathison, Keith A. *From Age to Age: The Unfolding of Biblical Eschatology.* Phillipsburg, NJ: P&R, 2009.

McDermott, Gerald R. *The New Christian Zionism: Fresh Perspectives on Israel and the Land.* Westmont, IL: InterVarsity, 2016.

McDowell, Josh, and Sean McDowell. *Evidence That Demands a Verdict, Life–Changing Truth for a Skeptical World.* Nashville, TN: Thomas Nelson, 2017.

Miller, Maureen C. "Bonds of Wool: The Pallium and Papal Power in the Middle Ages." *Church History* 87, no. 1 (2018) 198–200.

Miller-Naudé, Cynthia L., and Jacobus A. Naudé. "Textual Interrelationships involving the Septuagint Translations of the Precious Stones in the Breastpiece of the High Priest." *HTS Theological Studies* 76, no. 4 (2020) 1–16.

Morris, Leon L. *Revelation: An Introduction and Commentary.* Vol. 20. Downers Grove, IL: InterVarsity , 1987.

Mounce, Robert H. *The Book of Revelation.* Rev. ed. New International Commentary on the New Testament. Grand Rapids, MI: Eerdmans, 1997.

———. *The Book of Revelation.* Grand Rapids: Eerdmans, 1977.

Onion, Amanda. *Babylon.* https://www.history.com/topics/ancient-middle-east/babylonia.

Orr, James. "Eyesalve." *International Standard Bible Encyclopedia.* 1915. https://www.biblestudytools.com/dictionary/eyesalve/.

Osborne, Grant R. *Revelation Verse by Verse.* Oak Harbor, WA: Lexham, 2016.

———. *The Hermeneutical Spiral.* Downers Grove, IL: InterVarsity, 1991.

Padfield, David. *Colossae, Hieropolis, and Laodicea.* Nashville, TN: Thomas Nelson, 1982.

Pagels, Elaine. *Revelations, Visions, Prophecy, & Politics in the Book of Revelation.* New York: Penguin, 2012.

Podany, Amanda H. *Brotherhood of Kings: How International Relations Shaped the Ancient Near East.* England: Oxford University Press, 2012.

Ramsey, William M. *The Letters to the Seven Churches,.* Albany, OR: Books of the Ages, 1979.

Rappe, Donald. "Gathering Place for the End of Days." *Bible Today* 50, no. 6 (2012) 365–70.

Ratzabi, Hila. "What Is Gematria?" *MyJewishLearning.* March 7, 2002. https://www.myjewishlearning.com/article/gematria/.

Roberts, Alexander, and William Rambaut. "Ante-Nicene Fathers, Vol. 1." *New Advent.* Buffalo: Christian Literature, 1885.

Robinson, Andrew. "Identifying the Beast: Samuel Horsley and the Problem of Papal AntiChrist." *The Journal of Ecclesiastical History* 43, no. 4 (1992) 592–607.

Seiss, Joseph A. *The Apocalypse: Exposition of the Book of Revelation.* Grand Rapids, MI: Kregel Publications, 1987.

Siew, Tony. *The War Between the Two Beasts and the Two Witnesses: A Chiastic Reading of Revelation 11:1—14:5.* London: Bloomsbury, 2005.

Sproul, R. C. "The New Jerusalem." *Tabletalk Magazine,* August 1, 2020.

Stock, Markus. *Alexander the Great in the Middle Ages.* Toronto, Canada: University of Toronto Press, 2016.

Strauch, Alexander. *Love or Die, Christ's Wake-Up Call to the Church.* Littleton, CO: Lewis & Roth, 2008.

Svigel, Michael J. "The Phantom Heresy: Did the Council of Ephesus (431) Condemn Chiliasm?" *Trinity Journal* 24, no. 1 (2003) 105–12.

Sweet, J. P. M. *Revelation*. TPINTC. Philadelphia: Trinity, 1979.

Thomas, Robert L. *Revelation 8–22: An Exegetical Commentary*. Chicago: Moody, 1992.

Tiwald, Markus, and Jürgen Zangenberg. *Early Christian Encounters with Town and Countryside: Essays on Urban and Rural Worlds of Early Christianity*. Göttingen, Germany: Vanderhoeck & Ruprecht, 2021.

Tourist Israel. "History of Megiddo." *Tourist Israel: The Guide*. https://www.touristisrael.com/megiddo/9448/.

Trebilco, Paul. *The Early Christians in Ephesus from Paul to Ignatius*. Tübingen, Germany: Mohr Siebeck, 2019.

Trent, Council of. "Session 25." In *Bull of Our Most Holy Lord Pius IV., By Providence of God, Pope, Touching the Confirmation of the Oecuenical (and) General Council of Trent. 13 January, 1547*, edited by J. Waterworth, 232–89. London: Dolman, 1848.

Wiersbe, Warren. "Developing a Christian Imagination." In *Developing a Christian Imagination*, 21. Wheaton: Victor, 1995.

———. *Wiersbe's Expository Outlines on the New Testament*. Wheaton, IL: Victor, 1992

Wilcock, Michael. *The Message of Revelation: I Saw Heaven Opened*. Downers Grove, IL: Leicester, 1986.

Wilson, Christian J. "The Problem of the Domitianic Date of Revelation." *New Testament Studies* 39 (1993) 587–605.

Witherington, Ben, III. *Revelation—New Cambridge Bible Commentary*. Cambridge, UK: Cambridge University Press, 2003.

Woods, A. M. "Have the Prophecies in Revelation 17–18 about Babylon Been Fulfilled? Part 1." *Bibliotheca Sacra* 169, no. 673 (2012) 79–100.

———. "Have the Prophecies in Revelation 17–18 about Babylon Been Fulfilled? Part 3." *Bibliotheca Sacra* 169, no. 675 (2012) 341–61.

Wyk, Ignatius W. C. (Natie) van. "Philip Melanchthon: A Short Introduction." *Hervormde Teologiese Studies* 73, no. 1 (2017) 1–8.

Zuck, Roy B., and John F. Walvoord. *The Bible Knowledge Commentary: An Exposition of the Scriptures*. Edited by R. B. Zuck. Vol. 2. Wheaton, IL: Victor, 1985.